Comments on other *Amazing Stories* from readers & reviewers

"Tightly written volumes filled with lots of wit and humour about famous and infamous Canadians."
Eric Shackleton, *The Globe and Mail*

"The heightened sense of drama and intrigue, combined with a good dose of human interest is what sets Amazing Stories *apart."*
Pamela Klaffke, *Calgary Herald*

"This is popular history as it should be... For this price, buy two and give one to a friend."
Terry Cook, a reader from Ottawa, on **Rebel Women**

"Glasner creates the moment of the explosion itself in graphic detail...she builds detail upon gruesome detail to create a convincingly authentic picture."
Peggy McKinnon, *The Sunday Herald*, on **The Halifax Explosion**

"It was wonderful...I found I could not put it down. I was sorry when it was completed."
Dorothy F. from Manitoba on **Marie-Anne Lagimodière**

"Stories are rich in description, and bristle with a clever, stylish realness."
Mark Weber, *Central Alberta Advisor*, on **Ghost Town Stories II**

"A compelling read. Bertin...has selected only the most intriguing tales, which she narrates with a wealth of detail."
Joyce Glasner, *New Brunswick Reader*, on **Strange Events**

"The resulting book is one readers will want to share with all the women in their lives."
Lynn Martel, *Rocky Mountain Outlook*, on **Women Explorers**

GREAT CENTREMEN

AMAZING STORIES®

GREAT CENTREMEN

Stars of Hockey's Golden Age

HOCKEY

by Paul White

PUBLISHED BY ALTITUDE PUBLISHING CANADA LTD.
1500 Railway Avenue, Canmore, Alberta T1W 1P6
www.altitudepublishing.com
www.amazingstories.ca
1-800-957-6888

Extreme care has been taken to ensure that all information presented in
this book is accurate and up to date. Neither the author nor the
publisher can be held responsible for any errors.

Publisher	Stephen Hutchings
Associate Publisher	Kara Turner
Series Editor	Jim Barber
Editor	Deborah Lawson
Cover and Layout	Bryan Pezzi

We acknowledge the financial support of the Government
of Canada through the Book Publishing Industry Development
Program (BPIDP) for our publishing activities.

Altitude GreenTree Program
Altitude Publishing will plant twice as many trees as were used
in the manufacturing of this product.

Library and Archives Canada Cataloguing in Publication

White, Paul, 1950-
    Great centremen / Paul White.

    (Amazing stories)
    Includes bibliographical references.
    ISBN 1-55439-097-4

    1. Hockey players--Biography. 2. National Hockey League--Biography.
3. Hockey--Offense. I. Title. II. Series: Amazing stories (Canmore, Alta.)

GV848.5.A1H525 2006   796.962'092'2   C2005-906888-4

Amazing Stories® is a registered trademark of Altitude Publishing Canada Ltd.

Printed and bound in Canada by Friesens
2 4 6 8 9 7 5 3 1

To my wife, Judy.

Contents

Prologue

With only 39 seconds left in the game, the Toronto Maple Leafs trailed their arch rivals, the Montreal Canadiens, by a score of 2–1 in the 1951 Stanley Cup Final.

Desperate for a goal, the Leafs pulled goalie Al Rollins in favour of an extra attacker. The face-off was deep in the Canadiens' end. Veteran Toronto centre, Ted "Teeder" Kennedy stood at the face-off circle checking the positions of his teammates. His plan was to draw the puck back to fellow centre Max Bentley, who was playing the point.

Kennedy looked up to see that Montreal had sent out Billy Reay, their best centre, to take the face-off.

Better bear down, *thought Teeder.* Reay is a tough face-off man.

But before the linesman could drop the puck, the Montreal bench called for one last change.

When he saw the Montreal change, Kennedy couldn't believe his eyes! Elmer Lach was coming over the boards. Teeder had a long history with Lach. He was sure he could easily beat him on the draw.

The puck dropped. In the blink of an eye, Teeder swept

the puck back to Max Bentley. With a single swift motion, Bentley swung toward the net and fired the puck.

A black blur streaked straight for the net. But suddenly it seemed to change direction. In a flash, it shot behind a startled Gerry MacNeil into the Montreal net.

The score was tied!

They headed into overtime.

That was when Bill Barilko, a hard-hitting defenceman known more for his booming bodychecks than for his scoring prowess, netted perhaps the most mythical goal in the history of the Toronto Maple Leafs. It was the last goal Barilko would ever score ...

Introduction

Sports experts often state that the key to any successful team is strength down the middle. To win a Stanley Cup a team must have outstanding goaltending, solid defence, and exceptional centres on the forward lines.

A look at one of the most successful teams in the National Hockey League (NHL) during the past decade illustrates this truth. The Detroit Red Wings captured three Stanley Cups, finished first in the regular season several times, and most often went deep into the playoffs each season. Certainly they had stellar goaltending and all-star defencemen such as Chris Chelios, Nick Lidstrom, and Larry Murphy. But the players in their centre ice position probably made the difference most seasons. Perennial all-star and future Hall of Famer Steve Yzerman, accompanied by fellow centres Sergei Federov, Kris Draper, and now Pavel Datsuyk, led the way. In seasons when all three were healthy, the Red Wings dominated. But in years when injuries or other factors limited the play of these talented centres, Detroit failed in its quest for the Cup.

The men on whose careers we focus in this book were key to the success of their teams. But perhaps the adage concerning the power of "strength down the middle" is best illustrated by the three Toronto Maple Leaf centres who are featured here: Syl Apps, Ted "Teeder" Kennedy, and Max Bentley.

Conn Smythe, the Toronto Maple Leafs' owner and general manager, recognized the value of a strong core of players at centre position. He already had two of the best in Apps and Kennedy, but Smythe recognized that Apps was approaching retirement. Not wanting to be left without depth at this key position, he pulled off one of the largest trades in NHL history to acquire future Hall of Famer Max Bentley from Chicago.

Great centres are also great athletes. Alex Delvecchio and Sid Abel were named to the National Hockey League's All Star Team at two positions, centre and left wing. They joined Boston superstar Aubrey "Dit" Clapper as the only players ever to achieve this dual recognition. Jean Béliveau turned down a professional baseball career to pursue his dream of playing hockey. Milt Schmidt was also an above average baseball player. Syl Apps represented Canada in the

Olympics as a pole vaulter. Ironically, his hockey career with the Maple Leafs was assured when Conn Smythe watched Apps play football.

Many of the men featured in this book are proof that nice guys do finish first. Several of them were awarded the Lady Byng Trophy, for sportsmanship and gentlemanly conduct combined with performance in play. Several players won it more than once, and Frank Boucher received this trophy a remarkable seven times! On the occasion of the seventh Byng Award, the league retired the original trophy and presented it to Boucher.

Truly great centremen are not only great players but they also possess intangibles such as leadership. Consequently, it is no surprise that four of the men featured in this book — Ralph "Cooney" Weiland, Alex Delvecchio, Frank Boucher, and Milt Schmidt — were honoured with the Lester Patrick Award for their efforts to promote and develop the sport of hockey in the United States. Most of them became either coaches or general managers after their playing days came to an end. And all of them are honoured members of the Hockey Hall of Fame.

The last great hockey player featured in this book, Fred "Cyclone" Taylor, was not officially a centre. In his day, the sport of hockey featured seven men on the ice. The extra player was known as the rover. The rover's place on the ice wasn't clearly defined but, like a centreman, his responsibilities encompassed essentially the entire sheet of ice. Cyclone

Taylor was truly one of the best. In fact, some long-time sportswriters consider Taylor to be hockey's first superstar. From 1900 to 1918, he was named to the First All Star Team of every league in which he played.

Chapter 1
Sid Abel:
Old Bootnose

Hockey has been an important part of childhood for many youngsters growing up on the Canadian prairies. For Sidney Gerald "Sid" Abel, born in Melville, Saskatchewan, on February 22, 1918, hockey was the highlight of the long Canadian winters. As he and his friends skated on ponds, rivers, and backyard rinks, they dreamed of playing in the best hockey organization in the world, the National Hockey League.

Abel's dream of an NHL career took a step closer to reality when he began playing junior hockey with the Melville Millionaires of the Southern Saskatchewan Junior Hockey League. He split the 1936–1937 season with his hometown team and the Saskatoon Wesleys of the Northern Saskatchewan Junior Hockey League.

It wasn't long before his hockey talents attracted the attention of the many scouts who scoured the Canadian west looking for players for their NHL teams. Abel's professional hockey ambitions appeared to be headed for realization when Goldie Smith, the western Canadian scout for the Detroit Red Wings, signed the Melville teenager to a contract. All Abel had to do was go to training camp and impress Jack Adams, the Red Wings' coach and general manager.

With great anticipation, Abel reported to training camp where his play exceeded everyone's expectations. But nobody could find the contract Abel had signed, probably in the confusion surrounding the untimely death of scout Goldie Smith. When Jack Adams informed Abel that the club could not find his contract, Abel recalled wondering if he might be able to take advantage of the situation, thinking, "I could sign again for more money." Unfortunately, Abel's hopes for more money were dashed when Adams located the original contract.

Adams was uncertain whether the slightly built, 155-pound Abel had the stamina to withstand the pounding that the larger players would deal out to him during a long NHL season. But at his first Red Wings' training camp, Abel's outstanding play soon convinced Adams to overlook these physical limitations.

At the end of camp, the Red Wings' general manager wanted the youngster to remain in the southern Ontario-Michigan area and play for one of Detroit's farm clubs during the upcoming season. However, Abel declined the offer, choosing instead to play the 1937–1938 season in western Canada with the Flin Flon Bombers. The next season found Abel back at the Wings' training camp looking for a spot on the Wings' NHL roster.

This time his ambition was fulfilled, and Abel started his professional career in 1938–1939. But after 15 games with the Red Wings, despite seeming to fit into the NHL's scheme of things, he was sent to Detroit's American Hockey League farm club, the Pittsburgh Hornets, to further hone his hockey skills. At Pittsburgh he enjoyed a stellar season, scoring 21 goals and adding 24 assists. When he returned to the Wings' training camp the next season, he expected to land a position in Detroit. But, his expectations were not quite met; he split his second professional season, 1939–1940, between the Wings and their other top farm club, the Indianapolis Capitals.

In 1940–1941, Abel became a full-time member of the Detroit Red Wings. It did not take the young player long to demonstrate NHL-level hockey skills and leadership abilities. In his first full National Hockey League campaign, Abel's 11 goals were surpassed by only two teammates and his 33 points earned him the second highest total on the team.

In 1941–1942, Abel was the second highest Red Wings player in terms of both goals (18) and points (49). That season the young centre had been put on a line between two veteran wingers, Don Grosso and Eddie Wares. This line was given the unique moniker of the Liniment Line.

Sid Abel

Perhaps it was the stabilizing influence of his older wingers that enabled Abel to showcase his scoring talent and his abilities as a hockey player in general. Whatever the reason, he averaged one point per game during the regular season. One point per game may not seem like a great total in terms of present-day hockey statistics, but in the 1940s only the biggest stars of the league amassed scoring numbers at that level. The league recognized this stellar point production and his all-around excellent performance, naming him the centre on the league's Second All Star Team. (Ultimately, in fact, Abel's outstanding play resulted in his becoming one of only three men named to the NHL All Star Team at two positions. He was the Second All Star Team left winger in 1942 and the First All Star Team centre in both 1949 and 1950.)

After only two years as a full-time Red Wing, at the relatively young age of 24, Abel was named Detroit's captain. In his first campaign as captain, Detroit defeated Boston in four straight games to capture the Stanley Cup.

The season before Abel became captain, the Red Wings had thrown away a three-games-to-none series lead, losing the Stanley Cup to Toronto and becoming the first and only team in the history of the National Hockey League to lose the series in spite of having had such a commanding lead.

There were many reasons why Detroit lost the 1942 Stanley Cup series to Toronto. The inspired play of the Maple Leafs was an obvious major factor. But as well, the Red Wings, both players and coaching staff, lost their composure, allowing the Leafs to dictate the flow of the game. Coach and general manager Jack Adams was suspended for one game due to an attack on game officials. The Wings needed the calming influence of a strong leader to help them regain their focus on their goal: winning the Stanley Cup.

During the Stanley Cup playoffs the following season it was obvious that Detroit's new captain, Sid Abel, was not about to have history repeat itself. In the first game of the final series on April 1, 1943, the Red Wings' captain showed the way for his team. Abel notched four assists to tie the NHL record for assists in a Stanley Cup final game. He also tied the mark for total points in a final game. Detroit never looked back. After Abel's strong performance in the first game the team rolled over the Bruins to claim the Stanley Cup. This would be the first of three Stanley Cups (1943, 1950, and 1952) that would bear Abel's name as captain of the championship team.

After capturing the Stanley Cup in the spring of 1943, Abel put his career on hold, enlisting in the Royal Canadian Air Force (RCAF) during World War II. However, he did not see action in Europe. Instead, he spent most of the war in Quebec where he continued playing hockey. Although it was not the National Hockey League, he was still able to compete in the game he loved. In 1943–1944, Abel skated with the Royal Canadian Air Force hockey squad in Montreal, as well as a Montreal City League team called the Montreal Canada Car. The next season, the final year of the war (1944–1945), found Abel playing for the Lachine Rapides of the Quebec Provincial Hockey League as well as with the RCAF hockey squad in Kingston, Ontario.

In February 1946, at the age of 28, Abel returned to the Red Wings and played seven games at the end of the 1945–1946 season. However, his transition back to the professional game was not smooth. Although he had played hockey while in the armed forces, the level of play had not been equal to that of the National Hockey League. He had lost a step on some of the younger players and the strategy of the game had changed. But Abel worked hard; by the start of the 1946–1947 season he seemed to have found his stride again.

Meantime, Jack Adams spent most of that season trying to find a suitable combination of wingers for his returned captain. After a period of trial and error, Adams made a decision that would alter Abel's career and forever impact scoring in the National Hockey League.

During the latter half of the 1940s, the Red Wings had added many young players to their roster. Adams relied upon his veterans, led by Abel, to act as a calming force on the team. Among the youngsters who now skated with the Red Wings was a shy young man from Abel's home province of Saskatchewan, a right winger by the name of Gordie Howe. Another new winger, as pugnacious as Howe was shy, was Ted Lindsay. Both Howe and Lindsay were extremely talented hockey players with unlimited potential. To develop their skills, Adams decided to put them on the same line with his veteran captain at centre. Thus began the legendary Production Line, whose exploits would be etched into the record books of the National Hockey League as one of the greatest lines of all time.

The line probably received this moniker because Detroit (popularly known as Motor City) was the centre of the automobile industry, a place where production lines never shut down in order to meet North America's constant demand for cars. After all, the post-World War II era was one of constant economic growth and suburban sprawl, where the automobile was king.

Gordie Howe, in Dan Diamond's *Hockey: the Illustrated History*, said that the Production Line "used to pose on the assembly lines of the big Detroit auto plants." Howe also recalled, "Sid Abel used to say that he was 'the thinker,' who had to motivate me and slow Ted Lindsay down. We never started a year as a unit. They'd always split us up at the beginning, trying to spread the scoring around, but we'd end up together."

Abel was well-respected beyond the dressing room of his club. Along with Syl Apps of the Toronto Maple Leafs and Glen Harmon of the Montreal Canadiens, he was selected to represent NHL players at a September 1947 meeting of the NHL Board of Governors. The meeting was called to discuss the dispersal of gate receipts from the annual NHL All Star game. It was decided that the players' share would be put toward a pension fund. Previously that year it had been decided that the players would receive two-thirds of the All Star gate admissions.

In 1948–1949, Abel led the league with 28 goals and won the Hart Trophy as the league's Most Valuable Player. But the next season proved to be even more successful as he notched a personal best mark of 34 goals and 69 points. Abel was second only to his left winger, Ted Lindsay, who led the league in scoring. Their linemate, Gordie Howe, finished third. The league rewarded the players who finished first and second in the scoring race. To avoid unhealthy competition between the members of the Production Line, the three players decided they would share the bonus money equally, splitting it three ways.

Abel's nickname was Bootnose, a moniker he acquired because of a confrontation with Montreal Canadiens' Maurice "Rocket" Richard. In the Red Wings' first game against Montreal during Gordie Howe's rookie season, the young Howe collided with the volatile Canadiens superstar. Richard picked himself up from the ice and attacked Howe. The young Red Wing ducked, evading the punch, and landed one of his own to the Rocket's jaw. Hockey legend suggests that Abel taunted Richard, telling him that that would teach him not to fool with one of Detroit's rookies. An enraged Rocket rushed Abel, punching him in the nose. And what a punch it was! Abel's nose was broken in three places. Richard's wallop left its mark on his face — and landed him with an equally unforgettable nickname.

In the 1949–1950 playoffs the Red Wings faced the daunting task of defeating the two-time defending Stanley Cup champions, the Toronto Maple Leafs. As if a series between Toronto and Detroit needed any added spice, an unfortunate accident involving Detroit's young superstar Gordie Howe and Toronto's star centre Ted Kennedy provided even more drama for the fans and players.

The play started out quite innocently. Kennedy was skating along the boards, attempting to carry the puck up the ice into the Red Wings' end. As he neared the Wings' end, out of the corner of his eye he saw the hulking Howe steaming toward him. The rugged Red Wings player was coiled, ready to deliver a punishing bodycheck. At the last second, Kennedy ducked away from the thundering check. Howe, in an awkward freefall, tumbled headfirst into the boards.

The sickening thud of Howe's head against the boards sent a hush through the arena. Then pandemonium struck. Red Wings players, led by the volatile Ted Lindsay, rushed at Kennedy. Fights broke out all over the rink. Soon the ice was littered with wrestling blue- and red-jerseyed bodies. In the midst of the mayhem an injured Howe, blood oozing from his head, lay crumpled by the boards. Finally, cooler heads prevailed. The players returned to their benches while medical attendants rushed Howe to the hospital. Then the Red Wings' captain brought his team together, urging them to defeat the Maple Leafs — to win the Stanley Cup for their injured friend and teammate. And despite the loss of a star player and leading scorer, Abel and his teammates did just that.

Although the injury was considered severe, it wasn't until after the game that the players discovered Gordie Howe had been close to death. Years later, Abel would express regret over the way he and his teammates had roughed up Kennedy, conceding that the bodycheck thrown by the Leafs' player had probably not been an illegal one.

Sid Abel: Old Bootnose

At the end of the Red Wings' championship season of 1951–1952, Abel approached Jack Adams with a strange request. He wanted the Red Wings to trade him to the Chicago Blackhawks. Many wondered why anyone would want to leave Detroit, especially to go to the Windy City. After all, the Red Wings' team was loaded with veteran talent: The forward lines were deep with scorers; the defence was led by all-stars such as "Red" Kelly and Marcel Pronovost; in goal, the Red Wings boasted Terry Sawchuk, who would go on to become the greatest goalie of all time. Added to this veteran line-up were up-and-coming future Hall of Fame players like Alex Delvecchio. It certainly looked like the Red Wings would be a dominant force for years to come. The Blackhawks, in contrast, were a perennial last place team with little hope of upward mobility.

In fact, Abel's request stunned fans and teammates. It simply didn't make sense. The 1951–1952 season had been a dream that any player would have loved to experience, but few ever would. During the playoffs, Abel's Red Wings scored eight straight victories, allowing a grand total of only five goals against. Detroit had amassed in excess of 100 points for the second consecutive season, the first team to do so. This stunning plateau would not be reached again until the Montreal Canadiens duplicated the feat in 1968 (and even then, it could be argued that Montreal achieved this in a league that was considerably weaker because of expansion). No team had ever captured the championship in such an overwhelming manner.

Abel's reason for wanting a trade to Chicago was simple. He knew his years as a hockey player were numbered and he wanted to prepare for the future. The Blackhawks were looking for a new coach and they were prepared to allow him the dual role of player/coach. It seemed like the perfect opportunity.

Abel skated for the Blackhawks for two seasons. In his first season as player/coach with the hapless Blackhawks, Abel suited up for 39 games as a player. His scoring numbers declined dramatically from his Detroit days. Abel scored only five goals and four assists. The next season, 1953–1954, he played in only three games, and failed to score even a single point. This lack of scoring was probably one of the main reasons Abel retired as a player.

Not long afterward he returned to Motor City as a television analyst. Sid Abel later became coach, and eventually general manager, of the Detroit Red Wings.

Abel's love of the sport of hockey extended beyond his own career. He was keenly interested in developing the next generation of players. Gordie Howe recalled that Abel had been like a coach to him when they played together on the Production Line. On road trips, Howe recalled, Abel would sit with them and rehash the whole game, breaking it down like a coach and stirring up the players for the next game.

His contribution to hockey also extended, in a very direct way, beyond his own playing years. Sid Abel was the first of three generations of his family to play in the National Hockey League. His son Gerry played briefly with the Red Wings in the

1960s, and his grandson Brent Johnson is a goaltender who has played with the St. Louis Blues and the Phoenix Coyotes, and who now plays with the Washington Capitals.

Sid Abel was considered by many to be the backbone of the great Red Wings' teams of the late 1940s and early 1950s. Perhaps an indication of the respect given to him as a hockey player was seen in 1967 when his former linemate Gordie Howe was named the recipient of the Lester Patrick Award for outstanding contributions to hockey in the United States. Eleven hockey players were invited to the award dinner, as special guests, to honour Howe on the occasion of receiving this prestigious award. Six players — Bill Durnan, Doug Harvey, Rocket Richard, Milt Schmidt, Fern Flaman, and Doug Bentley — were selected as the All Star Team of Gordie Howe's opponents. The other five represented an All Star Team of Howe's teammates. They included goalie Harry Lumley, defencemen Bob Goldham and Bill Gadsby, left winger Ted Lindsay and, at centre, Sid Abel.

For most of Sid Abel's National Hockey League career as a centre — nine full seasons and parts of three other campaigns — the Detroit Red Wings were the favoured beneficiaries of his remarkable skill. The Production Line, which he centred, became one of the most famous lines in hockey history. Along with hockey legends Ted Lindsay and the incomparable Gordie Howe, Abel terrorized opposition goaltenders and led the Red Wings to many Stanley Cups and league championships.

In total, Abel spent more than five decades in the world of hockey as a player, coach, scout, general manager, and television commentator. And in 1969 Sid Abel was elected to the Hockey Hall of Fame, an honour reserved for only the greatest and most respected hockey players. In 1995 Abel received further recognition of his contribution to hockey when the Detroit Red Wings retired his #12 jersey and hung it from the rafters of the Joe Lewis Arena. It is displayed fittingly between the jerseys of #9 Gordie Howe and #7 Ted Lindsay.

Chapter 2
Syl Apps:
A World Class
Pole Vaulter

When one mentions the "prototypical" captain of a National Hockey League team, the first name that often comes to mind for long-time hockey fans is Syl Apps. Similarly, although Bobby Orr, Guy Lafleur, and Dave Keon are contenders for the title of the best skater in league history, once again, the choice of most experts is Syl Apps. With such commendations, it's hard to imagine that one NHL general manager decided not to sign him to a contract solely because Apps had aspirations of becoming a minister. Art Ross, coach and general manager of the Boston Bruins, originally scouted Apps. But Toronto

Maples Leafs' owner Conn Smythe, in his biography, *Conn Smythe: If You Can't Beat 'Em In The Alley*, co-authored by Scott Young, recalled Ross saying "… he was dammed if he wanted a minister on his team anyway." To further the irony, Smythe made the decision to hire Apps while watching him play football. He had to wait until hockey season to see Apps play hockey for the first time.

Sylvanus "Syl" Apps, alias "Slippery Sly" or "The Commish," was born in Paris, Ontario, on January 18, 1915. He played his entire professional career with the Toronto Maple Leafs.

Like most young Canadian boys, Apps may have spent his childhood dreaming of a career in the NHL. But he also spent a lot of time honing his athletic skills in other sports. Apps was an all-around athlete, playing hockey and football while he attended McMaster University. In his last year of university he played amateur hockey for the Hamilton Tigers.

But, long before Syl Apps became a household name in Canada, he had gained international recognition in a field completely unconnected with either of Apps' other two main sports. He was a world class pole vaulter. In 1934, Apps captured the Canadian and British Empire pole vaulting championship. The following year he successfully defended his Canadian title. Before turning professional as a hockey player, Apps represented Canada at the 1936 Olympics in Berlin, Germany, placing sixth among the world's elite vaulters.

When Apps joined the Maple Leafs in 1936 his hockey talents were immediately apparent. Apps wasted very little time establishing himself. In his first campaign he was recognized as an outstanding newcomer when he was awarded the Calder Trophy as the league's outstanding rookie. In fact, Apps was the first Maple Leaf to win this award.

When Apps joined the Leafs, Smythe tried him at centre on a line that was etched in Maple Leaf history as the famous Kid Line, between Charlie Conacher and Harvey "Busher" Jackson to fill the spot vacated by Joe Primeau's retirement. But that experiment didn't succeed. Expecting a rookie to replace the popular Joe Primeau between two established stars may have been too much to ask. The two veterans and their young rookie centre just did not mesh well as a unit.

The Leafs then tried Apps with another rookie, Gord Drillon, and the two youngsters immediately clicked. But they needed a complementing third linemate. Smythe added Bob Davidson, who had come up through the Leafs' minor hockey system, and immediately the trio became a highly effective unit, both offensively and defensively.

Apps' first season was an eye-opener for his team. The rookie notched 16 goals, an impressive number for that era in the National Hockey League. But even more astonishing was his assist total. He accumulated 29 assists, which was tops in the league. And as if to prove that his scoring exploits in his inaugural campaign were not a fluke, the league's Rookie of the Year had an even better second season. In the 1937–1938 season, Apps once again led the league in assists with 29, but he netted 5 more goals than in the previous season, for a total of 21.

Apps was a hard working but clean player, seldom putting his team at a disadvantage by taking penalties. In fact, Apps did not receive a single penalty during the entire 1941–1942 season.

But that season stands out in the long and storied history of the Toronto Maple Leafs for another reason. The Leafs captured the Stanley Cup in the most dramatic fashion ever witnessed in National Hockey League history.

The Detroit Red Wings opened the finals that season with three straight, decisive victories. It looked as if the Stanley Cup would be going to Motor City. The fourth, and what seemed certain to be the final, game was to be held in Detroit. With their backs to the wall the Leafs were desperate for a victory. In a 1975 interview with writer Jack Batten, Apps recalled the atmosphere in the Leafs' dressing room before that fourth game. "The only thing on our minds was, 'We can't go back to Toronto if we lose this game, too.' We were thinking we couldn't lose four straight and face the people back home."

The game was a hard fought, emotional contest, as each team took turns holding the lead. In the end, a third period goal by Toronto's Nick Metz clinched the 4–3 Leafs' victory. But the game was not without controversy. Detroit coach Jack Adams was upset by some of the referee's calls. In fact, he was so enraged that he barged into the referee's room at the end of the game, hurling insults at the officiating crew. For these actions, the league imposed a one-game suspension on Adams.

Detroit still held a commanding three-games-to-one series lead. But the Red Wings faced a combination of Adams' suspension, their emotional home ice loss in game four, and the injuries that a team accumulates during a long season and playoff run. Their momentum shuddered to an abrupt halt. In contrast, with that one do-or-die win under their belts, and Syl Apps' highly focused leadership, the Maple Leafs were on fire. They were not going to give in to Detroit without a fight.

The two teams returned to Toronto for the fifth game. The newly energized Leafs skated to a surprisingly easy 9–3 victory. Apps, centring a line with brothers Don and Nick Metz, led Toronto to victory with Don Metz scoring three goals. In the sixth game, back in Detroit, goalie Walter "Turk" Broda was the hero for the blue and white, shutting out the Wings for another Maple Leafs' victory.

The seventh game took the adversaries back to Toronto, where the whole city was hyped with Stanley Cup fever. A record crowd of 16,218 jammed into Maple Leaf Gardens to cheer on their heroes. For two periods it looked like Red Wings' goalie Johnny Mowers would spoil the Leafs' Cinderella comeback. But in the third period the Leafs roared back, scoring three unanswered goals. And with that, the 1942 Toronto

Maple Leafs accomplished a feat that has never been duplicated in the history of the National Hockey League. They
are the only team to ever lose the first three games of a final
series and then charge back with four straight wins to take the
Stanley Cup.

This dramatic Stanley Cup victory was engineered, in
large part, by their captain. Apps led all scorers in post-season
play that year. Although he scored only 5 goals, he amassed
a league-best 9 assists and captured the playoff scoring race
with 14 points. These numbers do not stand out compared to
today's playoff scoring feats, but in 1942 there were only two
playoff rounds compared to the four rounds played today.

Apps' skating abilities were legendary around the league.
He was not only a graceful skater, he was also very fast. The
rest of the National Hockey League caught a glimpse of how
speedy he was in 1942. "Moose" Ecclestone, a fastball player
in the Toronto area, had been injured. To raise funds to help
him out, the Leafs held a contest at Maple Leaf Gardens to
see who was the fastest skater in the league. Each NHL team
sent their fastest skater to compete. Apps easily defeated
great skaters like William "Flash" Hollett and Doug Bentley,
to claim the crown as the NHL's fastest man.

Apps was considered the consummate gentleman by
all who knew him, never swearing or drinking. When he
became extremely agitated over a situation he would express
his irritation or anger with such unseemly expressions as, "By
hum!" But this restrained attitude did not mean that Apps

allowed others to take advantage of his quiet nature. Early in his career, Boston defenceman William "Flash" Hollett high-sticked Apps, knocking out two of his teeth. Realizing that he had to make a statement, Apps promptly dropped his gloves and proceeded to give the surprised Hollett a severe beating. After that outburst, players around the league received the message and everyone steered clear of the Leafs' centreman.

Apps also seldom took bad penalties. During his 10-year NHL career he amassed a grand total of only 56 penalty minutes, which is less than three two-minute minor penalties a year.

Another example of App's honour and sense of fair play occurred during the 1942–1943 season. Apps broke his leg during a game. A week after the incident he hobbled into Smythe's office with a surprise for the Leaf's owner. According to Smythe, Apps handed him a cheque for $1,000, saying that he felt he shouldn't be paid until he could once again contribute to the team. Smythe declined his offer. Interestingly, that $1,000 cheque represented one-sixth of Apps' annual salary.

Before he broke his leg that season, Apps enjoyed one particular game that most players only dream about. On October 28, 1942, as the Maple Leafs played the New York Americans, the Toronto captain led the way for his team with six points. He had notched the hat trick in both goals and assists.

Apps missed the 1943–1944 and 1944–1945 National Hockey League seasons when he joined the Canadian Armed Forces during World War II. After he enlisted he was assigned to Smythe's Sportsmen's Battery. Before answering the call to fight for the freedom of his country Syl had achieved much success in the NHL. He captured the Lady Byng Trophy and the Stanley Cup in 1941–1942. He was named the league's All Star Centre twice and to the Second All Star Team three times.

He returned from the war in time to play for the Leafs in the 1945–1946 season. During the next three years he notched 24, 25, and 26 goals, leading Toronto to two more Stanley Cup victories.

Syl Apps retired at the end of 1947–1948 season with 201 goals, an average of 20 goals per season. It should be remembered that during the 1940s, a 20-goal season was the mark of truly superior goal scorer and hockey player. However, Apps didn't reach the 200-goal scoring plateau without a touch of drama. Entering the last game of the season he had tallied only 198 goals, two goals short of the impressive 200 mark. In that last regular season game of his career, Apps pulled off a hat trick to ensure his place in history. It was a truly remarkable feat. To cement his reputation as a winner, Apps led the Leafs to a Stanley Cup victory in his last season.

Conn Smythe said that the 1947–1948 team was the best Maple Leafs' team ever. Much of the reason for the greatness of the team was the fact that Smythe had three of the league's most remarkable centres in Syl Apps, Teeder Kennedy, and Max Bentley.

Apps was only 33 years old when he retired. According to teammate Sid Smith, "… he could have played another five or six years." Smythe regretted Apps' premature retirement for more than one reason. Obviously, the absence of this great centre hurt the team. But the Leafs' owner believed that Apps' departure from the game also probably shortened Teeder Kennedy's career. Kennedy tried to pick up the slack and, ultimately, tried to do too much. As great a player as he was, he couldn't be both Teeder Kennedy *and* Syl Apps.

Syl Apps has been recognized not only as one of the great hockey centres of all time, but also for his other athletic endeavours. He is an honoured member of the Hockey Hall of Fame, the Canadian Sports Hall of Fame, and the Canadian Amateur Athletics Hall of Fame. On October 3, 1993, the Toronto Maple Leafs hoisted a banner bearing the image of Syl Apps and his #10 jersey to the rafters of Maple Leaf Gardens.

Syl Apps' hockey legacy has continued since he retired from the game. His son, Syl Apps, Jr., enjoyed a career as a better-than-average player in the NHL with the Pittsburgh Penguins. His grandson played in the farm system of the Toronto Maple Leafs. Not to be outdone by the men in the family, Syl's granddaughter, Gillian, is a rising star in the National Women's Hockey League.

It could be argued that Apps comes from a family that has a strong tradition in hockey. Besides his own accomplishments and those of his direct descendants, two of his cousins, Murray Murdoch and Andy Blair, enjoyed long careers in the National Hockey League. Murdoch patrolled left wing for the New York Rangers from 1926 until 1937. Blair, who played centre for the Toronto club from 1928 until 1936, was traded to the Chicago Blackhawks just three months before Apps joined the Maple Leafs. Blair retired from the NHL after one season in the Windy City.

Syl Apps remained in the public eye after he left hockey. He was appointed the athletic commissioner for sports in the Province of Ontario in 1947. Apps later became a Conservative member of the Ontario Legislature, representing Kingston. While serving in the government of Ontario, he held the position of chairman of the Select Committee on Youth. In 1971 he gave up this post when he was appointed to the provincial cabinet as Minister for Correctional Services.

Chapter 3
Jean Béliveau:
A Gentleman and
a Hockey Player

s the two teams readied themselves for the opening face-off, Montreal fans roared their encouragement for the Habs, as the Montreal Canadiens were known (Habs is a shortened form of the French term, *habitant*). The Montreal Forum erupted with a massive cheer that echoed from every corner of the grand old building.

The puck dropped. Left winger Dick Duff grabbed it in the Chicago end. He spotted team captain Jean Béliveau in the open. In a flash, the flying disc was on Béliveau's stick. Just as quickly, the puck jetted in behind a startled Blackhawk goalie. Once again, a deafening din resounded throughout the Forum.

It was May 1, 1965. The Chicago Blackhawks and the

Canadiens were deadlocked at three games apiece in the Stanley Cup finals. Jean Béliveau's goal at the 14-second mark of the first period signalled that the Canadiens were not about to continue their five-year Stanley Cup drought.

Béliveau's goal proved to be both the game and the series winner. It was a repeat of Béliveau's performance in the spring of 1960, when another of his goals had won both the game and the Stanley Cup.

Hockey fans were never surprised when Béliveau scored an important goal. Throughout his legendary career, Béliveau was always at the centre of the action when it counted most. But, he was more than just a hockey player.

Jean Béliveau was a symbol, for his fans and his community, of what a star athlete should and could be.

Clarence Campbell, National Hockey League president from 1946 to 1977, once stated, "Any parent could use Jean Béliveau as a pattern or model. He provides hockey with a magnificent image. I couldn't speak more highly of anyone who has ever been connected with our game than I do of Jean."

Long before he suited up with the Montreal Canadiens, Jean Béliveau was already a legend in the hockey world. Throughout his junior career he was touted as the next "Great One" in hockey-mad Quebec.

Speculation about where he would play hockey provided fuel for an ongoing rivalry between Montreal and Quebec City. At first, Quebec City held sway. Despite the fact that Quebec City's hockey club played only in the Quebec Senior League,

Jean Béliveau

Béliveau enjoyed both fame and fortune playing in that community. Even more significant, perhaps, than the monetary rewards was the fact that Béliveau loved and respected the fans, who more than reciprocated his affection.

Béliveau was one of the most respected players in the history of the National Hockey League. The level of this respect is illustrated in a comment made by Gordie Howe, quoted in Lance Hornby's *Hockey's Greatest Moments.* Despite the nasty rivalry between the Red Wings and the Canadiens, Howe recalled that he would always shout, "Look out, Big Jean!" before he made contact, so Béliveau would be able to protect himself against injury from the bodycheck that was about to be delivered.

Béliveau's strong character was a result of his parents' influence. The eldest of Arthur and Laurette Béliveau's eight children, Jean Béliveau was born on August 31, 1931, in Trois-Rivières, Quebec.

When he was six years old his family moved to Victoriaville. Like countless Canadian families, each winter the Béliveaus skated on a backyard rink built by their father. Young Jean learned to skate and began honing his hockey skills under the watchful eyes of family.

He began playing organized hockey when he was 12 years old, in the Sacred Heart Academy house league. Three years later, Béliveau's skills were such that he not only played hockey for his school, but also suited up with the Victoriaville Panthers of the Intermediate "B" hockey league.

His parents were a consistent and steadying influence, helping their son make decisions concerning his hockey future. Béliveau recalled his father telling him, "No matter how many people will approach you with money and gifts and offers that seem ridiculously easy, you must remember that nothing comes free in this life, and that hard work and discipline will make you who and what you are." Anyone who takes the time to examine Béliveau's life, both on and off of the ice, will realize that his father's approach to life had a huge impact on him.

Béliveau's athletic abilities went beyond the hockey rink. In the summers he played baseball, dreaming of one day playing for his favourite team, the Boston Red Sox. His abilities as both a pitcher and a hitter attracted the attention of baseball scouts, and he was offered a contract to play in the southern United States. His mother, however, had other ideas. The thought of her eldest son going so far from home prompted her to refuse him permission to sign the contract.

In 1947, at the age of 16, Béliveau first came to the attention of NHL scouts. The coach of the Trois-Rivières junior team, who also scouted for the Toronto Maple Leafs, offered him the opportunity to sign a contract. But Jean's father turned down the offer, telling his son that there would be plenty of time to sign a contract. From that point forward, where and when he would play in the National Hockey League was a hot topic of conversation in Quebec and, indeed, throughout the entire hockey world.

The next season, 1948–1949, Béliveau scored a league-leading 48 goals for the Victoriaville Panthers intermediate team. His scoring abilities only further heightened the curiosity of hockey fans about where the 17-year-old would play next. The Montreal Canadiens made many attempts to sign Béliveau to a "C" form contract, which essentially tied a player to one team for the rest of his life. But, each time his father, who did not like the idea of signing a "C" form, rebuffed them. Finally, the Canadiens offered him a contract the family could accept.

But, that tie did not last long. Before the season started, a dramatic change occurred in Quebec junior hockey. The Montreal Canadiens provided the funds necessary to almost triple the number of teams in the league. Roland Hebert, coach of the new Victoriaville team, convinced the Canadiens to release Béliveau from his contract so he could play for his home team. Béliveau signed a one-year contract with Victoriaville. As events would transpire, one has to wonder if Montreal regretted their moment of largesse in releasing him from his first contract.

Young Béliveau rewarded his hometown fans with an outstanding season, winning both the Rookie of the Year award and the Most Promising Professional award.

But his stay with his hometown club would be short-lived. The next season, 1949–1950, he signed to play with the Quebec Citadels, for whom he scored 36 goals and 44 assists during the regular season. And in the playoffs, Béliveau demonstrated to the hockey world that he thrived in pressure situations, scoring a league-high 22 goals, and chalking up 31 total points.

At the beginning of the 1950–1951 season, Béliveau attended his first Canadiens' training camp. Before he left for Montreal, Frank Byrne of the Citadels told him they would match any offer made by the Canadiens. Byrne was wise to make such an offer. Béliveau won the league scoring title with 124 points, which included a league leading 61 goals. In the playoffs, once again Béliveau was a dominating force. He topped the league in scoring, with 23 goals and 54 points in only 22 games.

His popularity in Quebec City was immense. Some sportswriters began referring to the local arena as "Chateau Béliveau." During his first season there, he hosted a radio program for youngsters. This further promoted Béliveau's presence in the Quebec City area and deepened his connection with the community.

In December 1952 Béliveau joined the Canadiens for his second sojourn in the National Hockey League. His first game of the three-game stint was on December 18th against the New York Rangers at the Montreal Forum. If he had rookie jitters, it certainly didn't show. Béliveau netted three goals in a 6–2 Montreal victory. The other two games were a home and home series against the Boston Bruins. His electrifying performance, as he scored five goals in three games, proved once again that Béliveau was ready to play with the NHL's best. But, despite being named the Player of the Week, he returned to his faithful fans in Quebec City, leaving Montreal players and fans wondering when they would again see him wearing a Canadiens jersey.

The Rangers game provided Béliveau with a perfect view of the amazing Maurice "Rocket" Richard. For the first and only time, except on rare occasions and on power plays, Béliveau centred a line that featured the great Rocket on his right wing. That night against the Rangers, Richard — already known as a great scorer — proved to be a superior playmaker, assisting on all three of his rookie centre's goals.

While he remained in Quebec City, Béliveau's prowess as a hockey player was almost larger than life. Fans and sportswriters alike constantly discussed which combination of wingers would best suit his style when he finally joined the Canadiens. Some suggested Rocket Richard. Others promoted the idea of putting a young winger on Béliveau's right flank, a player with a booming shot by the name of Bernie "Boom Boom" Geoffrion. When Béliveau's fans weren't watching him play, they were talking about him. He was an endless source of conjecture.

At the end of Béliveau's junior career, Quebec City fans surprised their young hero with a special night. Among the honours and gifts bestowed upon him was a new 1951 Nash automobile.

This sentiment between Béliveau and his fans proved to be reciprocal. Rather than turning professional with the Canadiens, he opted to play senior hockey with the Quebec Aces. His decision was, in part, a way of showing his gratitude to the fans of the community.

The Canadiens, who'd been looking forward to having the budding superstar in their line-up, were upset at losing him to the senior club. So an attempt was made to change the Canadian Amateur Hockey Association's rules regarding graduating junior players. The proposed new regulation stated that any player on a National Hockey League negotiation list had to sign a contract with that team. If the player wanted, instead, to play senior hockey, the senior team would have to strike a deal with the NHL club that held the player's rights. It appeared to most people that this new rule was directed specifically at Jean Béliveau and the Quebec Aces, so it became known as the "Béliveau Rule." Fortunately for the Aces and Béliveau, it was never enacted.

Although Béliveau felt an obligation to the Quebec fans, he was also extremely well paid to stay in Quebec City. The Aces paid Béliveau $10,000 in 1951–1952, his rookie season in the Quebec Senior League. While this may not seem like a lot of money compared to present-day NHL salaries, the standard pay scale in the NHL during the early 1950s was about $100 per game which, calculated over a full season, was about $7,000.

The Aces were well rewarded for the generous salary that they paid to Béliveau. In his rookie season he won the league's scoring title with 83 points and topped the loop with 45 goals. Béliveau once again shone in the playoffs with a league best 14 goals in 15 games.

His salary the next season jumped to $20,000. In his autobiography, *Jean Béliveau: My Life in Hockey*, he wrote, "… for a short time, I was making more than Gordie Howe and Maurice Richard." Once again, he proved his worth to the club by capturing the league scoring title with 89 points. Béliveau netted 5 more goals than he'd scored in his rookie season, topping the best snipers in the league with 50 goals in 57 games. With 29 playoff points he dominated post-season play.

Throughout his playing time in Quebec City, media across the province and indeed in many Canadian and American hockey towns speculated about the reasons why Béliveau preferred to stay in semi-professional hockey rather than skate under the bright lights of the NHL arenas. More often than not, especially in Montreal, the media wrote about the money that he was making. However, in his autobiography Béliveau revealed his reasons for staying in Quebec. His decision, he said, was only partly about the game of hockey. Instead, he said, "I stayed in Quebec City, first and foremost, out of a sense of obligation to the people." Béliveau also stated that "the extra time in Quebec, as it turned out, helped me acclimatize to the demands of city life and to grow up more normally — or at least more gradually and in a more orderly fashion — than I would have had I been a twenty-year-old Montreal Canadien."

He said that because of his time in Quebec when he "finally did sign with Montreal … [he] was much better prepared for the demands of NHL stardom."

On October 3, 1953, the speculation finally came to an end as the Montreal Canadiens inked the coveted Béliveau to a contract to play in the National Hockey League. General Manager Frank Selke is reported to have said, "We just opened up the vault and said, 'Jean, take what you think is right.'"

Montreal had gone to extreme lengths to ensure that Béliveau would wear the red, white, and blue jersey of the

Canadiens. They simply bought the whole Quebec Senior League. In doing so, the Montreal team acquired every player in the league. The new owners made a professional league out of it, calling it *La Ligue Senior Professionelle du Quebec.* Béliveau did not have any other choice than to join the Canadiens. The athlete from Victoriaville, who was by then 23 years old, received a $20,000 bonus when he signed his first contract on October 3, 1953. Moreover, "Grand Jean" was assured of a $105,000 salary, spread over five years.

Béliveau's decision to play in Montreal actually may have been hastened by an event that occurred a season earlier when Zotique Lesperence, vice-president of Public Affairs, approached him about performing public relations duties for Molson Brewery. After the season ended, Jean agreed to work for the company. He went to Montreal to train for his position and also signed with the Canadiens. Little did he realize that this relationship with Molson's would last long after he retired from hockey, and that the training he received would stand him in good stead both in and out of the world of sports.

Béliveau's first season with the Canadiens probably did not live up to the expectations of the fans who had so eagerly awaited his arrival in the NHL. In 44 games he scored only 13 goals and 21 assists. But in the playoffs he once again showed his superb skills, leading all players with eight assists. And in the next season, 1954–1955, Béliveau's scoring totals were more what the Montreal faithful had hoped for, as he notched 37 goals and 36 assists in 70 games.

In Béliveau's third season with the Canadiens he was a commanding presence. He led the league with 47 goals and won the scoring title with 88 points. And in the playoffs he led the way with 19 points, including 12 goals, as the Canadiens won the first of what would be five successive Stanley Cups. Throughout that five-year span, Béliveau was consistently near the top of the league in scoring, including an impressive 45 goals in 1958–1959.

The Canadiens' Stanley Cup victory of 1960 marked the end of an era for the Canadiens. Maurice Richard retired. The team had gotten old during its five-year Cup dominance.

When the Canadiens traded captain Doug Harvey to the New York Rangers in 1961, Béliveau was elected by his teammates to succeed him. However, Béliveau's selection did not come without controversy. As one of the most senior players on the club, Boom Boom Geoffrion had expected to succeed Harvey. When Béliveau discovered his teammate's feelings were hurt he offered to give up the "C", but the team's management told him he was captain.

The captaincy mantle of the Canadiens was not an easy burden to shoulder. Montreal had won so many Stanley Cups, including five in a row to end the 1950s, that the fans had come to expect victory every season. When the string of Cups did not continue there was much grumbling in the stands, bars, and streets of the province of Quebec.

As the club entered the 1964–1965 playoffs the fans grew even more anxious. The Habs had finished second to the Detroit Red Wings by a mere four points. They opened the first round of the playoffs against the Maple Leafs. After winning a six-game series with Toronto, Montreal faced Chicago in the finals. The question fans and media were asking was whether the team could finally win the Cup again.

The series was evenly matched, with each team claiming victory on home ice. With the series tied at three games apiece, the two rivals faced off at the Montreal Forum for game seven on May 1, 1965.

Both the fans and the players were hungry for victory. As the game was about to begin the hometown fans sent up a huge roar for their heroes. Perhaps this outpouring of support boosted the Canadiens.

From the opening face-off, the Canadiens moved into the Blackhawks' end. Dick Duff had the puck. In a flash the left winger delivered a beautiful pass to Béliveau and before the fans could settle into their seats, they were on their feet with a tumultuous roar. Just 14 seconds gone in the game, and the captain had scored.

The tone of the game had been set. The Canadiens were relentless. They skated and they scored. At the end of the first period the bewildered Blackhawks headed to their dressing room on the wrong end of a 4–0 score. They knew they had a formidable task ahead of them if they were going to make a game of it.

During the next two periods, despite the Blackhawks' frantic efforts, the score remained the same. Shortly after the final buzzer, Jean Béliveau hoisted the Stanley Cup for the first time as the captain of the Montreal Canadiens.

The next season, Montreal once again faced the Maple Leafs in the semifinals; just as in the previous season, they defeated their bitter rivals. Perhaps they were a bit too sure of themselves as they opened the 1965–1966 Stanley Cup finals against the Detroit Red Wings on home ice. The Wings surprised them, winning both games to take a two game series lead. The Canadiens were determined to stave off defeat. The club pulled together and swept the next four games to capture a second straight Stanley Cup.

During the 1966–1967 season Béliveau incurred an injury that almost ended his career. In a game against Chicago, he was battling for the puck with Doug Jarrett and Stan Mikita when the blade of a stick creased his eyeball. He was rushed to the hospital but it was three days before the doctors were able to determine the full extent of the injury. Béliveau was very worried that he would lose his sight in the eye. After nine days in the hospital and five weeks out of the line-up, he worried about whether he would be able to play without fear once he returned to action. Béliveau need not have worried. He just picked right up where he left off.

Béliveau's only other physical limitation occurred in the early 1960s when he suffered from chronic fatigue. It was revealed that his heart was too small in relation to the size of the rest of his body. According to sportswriter Paul Rimstead, the comment at the time had been that "Béliveau had a

Model T heart in a Cadillac body." The main consequence of this discovery was that Jean had to have a cardiogram every year. Although the press discovered this ailment in the 1960s, both Jean and the Canadiens' doctors had been aware of the condition since he signed his contract with the club in 1953. It had been uncovered when the Canadiens had tried to obtain insurance on him after signing a $100,000 contract. General Manager Frank Selke was stunned when the insurance company refused to issue a policy. Although the condition was not life threatening, it was one that might have led many others to find another line of work. Béliveau just ignored it, continuing on in the career he loved.

However, by the 1961–1962 season Béliveau was extremely fatigued. He went to the Leahy Clinic in Boston for tests. There, doctors were amazed that he could function as an athlete at all, but assured him he was not at risk to continue playing.

Despite the fact that he played in 10 Stanley Cup championships and many more playoff games, Béliveau scored only one overtime goal during his entire NHL career. The dramatic moment took place in the 1968–1969 semifinals against the Boston Bruins. In the 91st minute of the sixth game Claude Provost won a battle for the puck along the boards. He quickly passed to Béliveau who fired the puck into the upper corner of the net behind Gerry Cheevers, clinching the game and the series.

Béliveau entered his retirement from hockey in style.

His last game was played in Chicago on May 18, 1971. On that evening, at the end of the game, Montreal Canadiens' captain Jean Béliveau hoisted the Stanley Cup above his head and led his team in a victory lap around Chicago Stadium. It was Béliveau's astounding 10th Stanley Cup, second highest in NHL history, behind his teammate Henri Richard's 11.

Béliveau retired as the all-time leading scorer in the history of the Montreal Canadiens franchise. As well, he was a 10-time all-star (six times a member of the First All Star Team) and the leading scorer in Stanley Cup history. He captained the Canadiens for 10 years. Béliveau captured the Art Ross Trophy as the league's leading scorer in 1955–1956. The Hart Trophy for the NHL's Most Valuable Player (MVP) was awarded to him on two occasions, 1955–1956 and 1963–1964, and he was the first winner, in 1964–1965, of the Conn Smythe Trophy as the Most Valuable Player in the Stanley Cup playoffs. On January 23, 1956, Jean Béliveau became the first hockey player to appear on the cover of *Sports Illustrated*.

Béliveau announced that he planned to retire at the end of the 1970–1971 season. On March 24, 1971, the club held a special night in his honour. He told the Canadiens that he did not wish to receive any gifts, but that money could be donated to charity in his name. Much to his surprise, on the evening of the special presentation Béliveau was given a cheque for $155,855. This created the funds necessary to finance the creation of the Jean Béliveau Fund. For the next two decades the fund grew, and Jean was able to contribute to many charitable organizations. When he retired as an executive of the Canadiens, Béliveau gave the remaining funds in the trust, $900,000, to the Quebec Society for Disabled Children. It was designated for use at a summer camp near Joliette.

In the *Star Weekly Canadian Magazine*, Paul Rimstead interviewed several Canadiens players in an article about Béliveau entitled, "The best that ever came down the pike." John Ferguson told Rimstead, "What can you say about the guy? He just has so much class, on and off the ice. And he never says anything bad about anybody." Another Canadiens teammate, Dick Duff said, "It's his quiet dignity. Jean is so unassuming for a guy of his stature."

Rimstead wrote that everybody on the Canadiens wanted to play with Béliveau. Many argued that his goal totals could have been much higher, but he more often than not chose to pass the puck to one of his wingers. When Dick Duff arrived in Montreal after being traded by the Rangers, he discovered that he would be playing on Jean's left wing. He asked Béliveau if there was anything he wanted him to do. Béliveau's response was simple, "Just play."

Perhaps Hector "Toe" Blake, the legendary Canadiens player and then coach, best described Jean Béliveau in a quote in Claude Moutons' book, *The Montreal Canadiens*. Blake said, "Ever since Béliveau has been associated with hockey … I have never heard any derogatory comments about him. As a hockey player and a gentleman, Jean Béliveau is unbeatable … He has no equal."

Chapter 4
Max Bentley: The Dipsy Doodle Dandy of Delisle

Max Bentley failed auditions with two National Hockey League clubs, and when he was finally inked to a contract it was for a position with a minor club belonging to the woeful Chicago Blackhawks. Yet a few years later he would be the key player in one of the largest trades in NHL history. Max Bentley went from being unwanted to being the focus of attention for a man known for his shrewd sense of hockey talent — Conn Smythe of the powerful Toronto Maple Leafs.

Max Bentley was born on March 1, 1920, in Delisle, Saskatchewan. He was one of 13 children. Hockey was an important pastime for the children in the Bentley home when Max was growing up. Like most Canadian youngsters, his childhood winters were spent skating on frozen ponds, rivers, and outdoor rinks. The long hours of skating in sub-zero weather on the windswept Canadian prairies paid off for Max and his brothers. At one time, Max and four of his five brothers all played for the same team, the Drumheller Miners.

Bentley's scoring prowess with Drumheller soon drew the attention of scouts. In his first season with the Miners he scored 28 goals in 26 games. The following year he notched 29 goals in 32 games. Playing for the Saskatoon Quakers, he led the league in scoring with 37 goals in 31 games in his last year as an amateur, following which he attended his first professional training camp.

Despite spending his youth enduring harsh prairie winters, Bentley was a frail youngster who only weighed 145 pounds when he was discovered by the Boston Bruins and attended his first training camp. Without a doubt he dreamed of playing in the National Hockey League against his older brother Doug, who was with the Chicago Blackhawks. But his experience at the Bruins' camp was very disappointing. Probably because of his frail-looking appearance and small stature, Bentley was virtually ignored by the coaches and management, and he was sent home without a contract or the promise of a future in hockey.

Undeterred by this setback, on his way home from the Bruins' camp Bentley went to Montreal's training camp to see about a tryout with the Canadiens. But when he was given a physical examination, the Montreal team doctor told him that he had a heart condition and should find a career outside of hockey. The doctor considered his heart condition to be so severe, he cautioned the youngster that if he didn't forget about hockey he would probably not live another year.

But the desire to play hockey in the National Hockey League burned so strongly in Bentley that, despite the ominous threat of the Montreal doctor, he took his fragile body to Chicago to seek a tryout there. The Blackhawks, whose roster consisted largely of cast-offs from the other teams, were perennial cellar-dwellers in the NHL. However, there were some quality players on the team, including Bentley's brother, Doug. That same season another Bentley brother, Reg, suited up with the Blackhawks for 19 games, scoring one goal and two assists. It seemed fitting that Max Bentley, who had been rejected by two other NHL clubs, would receive a contract offer from the lowly Blackhawks.

However, the Blackhawks decided that Max should first go to their farm club in Kansas City to further develop his skills — and perhaps put on a few pounds to help him withstand the NHL's punishing play. Initially, Bentley was inclined to "retire" at the young age of 18, rather than report to the minors. But former NHL player Johnny Goetselig, a childhood hero of Bentley's, was the coach in Kansas City. Goetselig promised Max that he would look after him and get him to the NHL as quickly as possible. Reluctantly, the youngster agreed. Shortly after Bentley joined the Kansas City team, the Blackhawks contacted Goetselig, asking him to send up a forward. Bentley had played well for the Kansas City team, scoring five goals and five assists in five games. True to his word, Goetselig rewarded Bentley for his efforts. The young man found himself headed for Chicago and the National Hockey League.

It was all he needed. The youngster from the prairies immediately blossomed into a big league star. Playing with his brother Doug and Harold "Mush" Marsh on a line dubbed the Pony Line, the trio brought some respectability to the last place Blackhawks. The next season, 1942–1943, Bill Mosienko replaced Marsh on the line with the Bentley brothers. This move proved to be the turning point for Max and Doug. Doug won the scoring title. And not far behind, in third place, was little brother Max, with 26 goals and 44 assists for 70 points. This point total, in conjunction with only two minutes in penalties, helped him capture the Lady Byng Trophy. Bentley's line provided Chicago fans with something to cheer about in hockey's wasteland in the 1940s.

Bentley's physical frailties followed him throughout his career. He was constantly plagued with minor injuries and ailments. Bentley suffered from dry throat, burning eyes, and upset stomach. He also contracted major disabilities such as diabetes and kidney problems. These ailments became so prominent in his daily life that some people referred to him as "a walking drug store."

Despite this, Max was known throughout the league for his skating and scoring prowess, his ability to drive to the net, and a style of play in which he seemed to be in constant motion (and which was probably responsible for his descriptive nickname, the Dipsy Doodle Dandy of Delisle). Max was also big on determination. In 1945–1946, his commitment to the game saw him score 31 goals and earn 30 assists. His 61 points were tops in the National Hockey League that year, garnering Bentley his first scoring title.

The following season he was involved in a dramatic scoring race with none other than the legendary Rocket Richard. With one game remaining in the 1946–1947 regular season, Bentley was one point ahead of Richard in the scoring. The Blackhawks had one game remaining against the Rangers, while Richard and the Canadiens were facing the Bruins. The game was essentially meaningless to the final league standings, as the Blackhawks were mired in their usual residence — the league's basement. Still, a scoring title would be something for the Chicago fans to cheer about.

By the end of the second period, the Rangers had held Bentley scoreless. Not so for his Montreal rival. Bentley received a report that the Rocket had notched two points, taking a one-point edge in the race. Then, early in the third period Max assisted on a Blackhawk goal. The point moved him into a tie with Richard. At the midway point of the third period, Bentley scored on a pass from Bill Mosienko to move into the lead once again. Richard failed to garner a point in the third period of his game. Bentley had captured his second consecutive scoring title.

Max Bentley: The Dipsy Doodle Dandy of Delisle

Bentley was awarded the Hart Trophy as the league's Most Valuable Player in 1945–1946. He captured the Art Ross Trophy as the league's scoring champion in both 1945–1946 and 1946–1947. One has to wonder what the brain trusts in Montreal and Boston were thinking about the hockey player they'd deemed unfit for a career in the National Hockey League.

Despite Bentley's terrific play, Chicago remained the league doormat. Although the Blackhawks iced as many skaters each night as their opponents, their talent pool was decidedly lacking in depth. Near the beginning of the 1947–1948 season an opportunity arose that would allow them to improve the overall strength of the club. But it would cost them perhaps their greatest asset. After weighing their options, on November 2, 1947, Blackhawks' management pulled the trigger on a huge trade.

They sent Bentley and Cy Thomas to Toronto in a block-buster swap that saw the Blackhawks receive five players in return. The Leafs sent the Blackhawks an entire line: Bud Poile, Gaye Stewart, and Gus Bodnar (affectionately named the "Flying Forts" in honour of their home town Fort William, Ontario), as well as veteran defencemen Bob Goldham and Ernie Dickens.

Not only did Conn Smythe pay a steep price to acquire Bentley, one of the best centres in the game, but the number of players involved in the transaction was a National Hockey League record up to that point.

But Smythe had his reasons. The Leafs' star centre, Syl Apps, would be retiring soon. The Bentley trade was made to ensure continuity of depth down the middle. And deep the Maple Leafs were!

Syl Apps centred the first line, with Harry Watson and Bob Davidson on the wings. The second line featured Teeder Kennedy between Vic Lynn and Howie Meeker. Bentley, a scoring champion and league Most Valuable Player, found himself centring the third line. In the history of the National Hockey League there may have been no better third line centre on any team, except perhaps the annual All Star Team. Bentley's arrival in Toronto gave both the team and its fans hopes of invincibility. And perhaps these feelings were well-founded. The trade made Conn Smythe look like a genius, as the Leafs with Bentley won three Stanley Cups in the next four years.

The 1947–1948 Stanley Cup final series against the Detroit Red Wings illustrated the impact of the Maple Leafs' tremendous offensive depth.

The Leafs won the first two games of the series on home ice by close scores, 5–3 and 4–2. In the third game of the series, they went to Detroit and shut out the Red Wings 2–0 in their own arena. In the fourth and, as it turned out, final game, the Leafs pummelled Detroit 7–2 to capture the Stanley Cup.

At the forefront of Toronto's stunning sweep of the finals was their vaunted trio of talented centres. Kennedy, assisted by Bentley, scored Toronto's first goal on a power play.

Max Bentley

Kennedy netted another marker while Apps scored a goal and his line notched two others. Meanwhile Bentley earned two assists. The Leafs were so deep in talented forwards, the Wings could not cover them all. The result was that if they stopped one line, another line picked up the slack and provided the offensive firepower.

One night at Maple Leaf Gardens the Leafs were in desperate need of a goal. Charlie Hempstead, a racehorse owner who held season tickets to Leafs' games and sat next to the Toronto bench, told Bentley that if he scored a goal he would give Bentley a racehorse. Bentley obliged the Leafs' patron and, in due course, received the promised racehorse.

In the 1951 Stanley Cup finals, Bentley played an integral part in one of the most famous goals in the history of the Stanley Cup. With less than a minute remaining in the third period the Leafs were down by one goal to Montreal. The face-off was deep in the Canadiens' end. As Teeder Kennedy prepared for the puck drop, he checked the positioning of his teammates. In particular, he wanted to be sure that he knew where Bentley was on the point.

As the puck left the linesman's hand, Kennedy went into action. His stick was little more than a blur as he whipped at the puck. The black disc flashed onto Bentley's stick. The Dipsy Doodle Dandy moved quickly toward the net, adeptly positioning himself for a shot. He fired a bullet. At the last second the puck was deflected, changing direction and bulging the twine behind a startled Montreal net minder. The game was tied and the teams were headed to overtime.

In overtime, Toronto's bashing blueliner, Bill Barilko, scored for the Maple Leafs to win the game and the Stanley Cup.

This goal and the man who scored it, however, have become legends unto themselves in the folklore of the Toronto Maple Leafs. Barilko, who was better known for dishing out punishing bodychecks than for his scoring touch, would never play another NHL game. That summer he disappeared while on a fishing trip in Northern Ontario. It would be more than a decade before his remains and the plane in which he crashed were found. Ironically, the Toronto Maple Leafs were unable to win another Stanley Cup until 1962, the same year Barilko's body was recovered.

But if it had not been for the shot fired by Max Bentley with only 39 seconds remaining in the game, Bill Barilko would probably never have scored his mythical goal.

During the 1952–1953 season Bentley was forced to retire. The story around this retirement is one of mystery and intrigue. In early March 1953 he was suffering from a back injury. One day he checked out of his hotel and disappeared, without telling anyone where he was going or what he was up to. When the Leafs failed to hear from Bentley, they contacted the authorities. A check at the border revealed that he had crossed into the United States at Port Huron, Michigan, taking the popular shortcut across the northern American states, then headed back into Saskatchewan. The Leafs figured he must have been heading home to Delisle.

Once Max arrived at his parents' home, he contacted Conn Smythe and told the Leafs' owner that he would rest up, and then return to Toronto for the playoffs.

On August 11, 1953, the Leafs sold his rights to the New York Rangers. The temptation to once again play with his brother, Doug, enticed Max to lace up his skates one more time. Bentley's scoring totals were not up to his career standard. In 57 games he scored only 14 goals and 18 assists for a meager 32 points. Bentley retired from the National Hockey League at the end of the season.

Although two NHL clubs, the Boston Bruins and the Montreal Canadiens, decided not to sign Bentley to a contract, he went on to prove all his detractors wrong. His awards included the Lady Byng Memorial Trophy, the Art Ross Trophy, and even, despite playing for the woefully inept Chicago Blackhawks, the Hart Memorial Trophy as the league's Most Valuable Player in 1945–1946. He was an NHL leading scorer and a member of both the First All Star Team and the Second All Star Team. But the ultimate hockey achievement for Max Bentley, the undersized, physically small centreman, was his induction as an honoured member of the Hockey Hall of Fame.

Chapter 5
Frank Boucher: The One-Fight Wonder

Frank Boucher's life revolved around the world of hockey. He was a Hall of Fame player, coach, and manager. Frank Boucher was an innovative thinker, both as a player and a member of management. As a coach, he was the first to pull a goalie during play rather than wait for a face-off. As chairman of the NHL Rules Committee, he used his vast knowledge and experience to rewrite the rule book that governs the game today.

Frank "Raffles" Boucher was born in Ottawa, Ontario, on October 7, 1901. Although he possessed a French name, Boucher's father, Tom, spoke very little French. In fact, it was Frank's Irish mother, Annie, who was fluently bilingual!

Tom Boucher was a large man weighing nearly

250 pounds. He was an accomplished football player who suited up with some great teams in the Ottawa area that won national championships. Ironically, one of his football teammates was Tom Clancy, father of the legendary hockey player, coach, and referee, Francis "King" Clancy. There were six boys and two girls in the Boucher family. Frank and his brothers grew up skating on backyard rinks and local ponds.

The first pair of skates Frank Boucher owned were given to him by his brother's friend. They were only skate blades and he had to find his own boots for them. Finally, Boucher took an old pair of hand-me-down football shoes that had been worn by several of his brothers. He had a difficult time screwing the blades into the bottom of the worn out shoes. But, at last, he had skates. The bottoms of the shoes were so worn out that the screws would come out of the boot while he was skating, and the blades would fall off. He would have to go home and put them back together.

The pool of young talented hockey players striving for a professional career must have been very deep. Among the many youngsters who played hockey on one of Boucher's school teams was his winger, Aurel Joliat. Joliat would go on to become a star player with the Montreal Canadiens playing on the wing of a line centred by the immortal Howie Morenz. Like his childhood friend, Boucher, Joliat's skills as one of the great players in the NHL would result in his induction to the Hockey Hall of Fame. But the talent pool began with Frank's own family. The Boucher boys were obviously skilled players. At one time in the 1920s, four of them were playing professional hockey. George was with the Ottawa Senators, Billy and Bob skated with the Montreal Canadiens, and Frank played for Vancouver.

Frank played junior hockey with the Ottawa New Edinburghs when he was 15 years old. After two years with them, he joined the senior version of the same team.

At the age of 17, Frank decided he needed to have a career beyond hockey so he joined the Royal North West Mounted Police and was posted in Regina. But he couldn't quite forget about hockey. When his brother Billy went to Iroquois Falls to play hockey and work at the local paper mill, he encouraged Frank to quit the Mounties and join him there. Boucher borrowed the $50 necessary to buy his way out of the force and headed east. He later recalled that it took him a year to pay back the debt.

However, before he started to play in Iroquois Falls, Boucher was offered an opportunity to fulfill his childhood dream of playing professional hockey. When Tommy Gorman offered him $1,200 a year to turn professional with the Ottawa Senators for the 1921–1922 season, he jumped at the offer.

That first year in the big league proved to be a disappointment. Boucher sat on the bench for the entire season seeing only spot duty, with the exception of one game. His fellow benchwarmers included future Hall of Famer and childhood friend King Clancy. The term "benchwarmer" was ironic, because in the unheated arenas they nearly froze waiting for the opportunity to go on the ice. In this era, the starting players played most of the game. Substitutes were seldom called upon unless one of the starters was injured. Because the arenas were unheated, the substitute players asked Gorman if they could sit in the heated dressing room waiting to be called to substitute.

At first he refused to consider the request. But, Gorman finally relented when the players created a plan to have a system of buzzers to call someone to substitute. Each player was designated by a number of buzzes. For example, if the coach needed Clancy he would buzz once and if he wanted Boucher he would press the buzzer twice. The first time Boucher was called to play he scored three goals.

Boucher had replaced his hero, Frank Nighbor. Nighbor was one of hockey's early superstars. In 1924 he captured the Hart Trophy as the league's Most Valuable Player. It is obvious that Nighbor's style of play had a huge impact on Boucher. In 1925 and again in 1926, Nighbor was awarded the Lady Byng Trophy, an award that would virtually become Boucher's personal property a decade later. As well, Nighbor would become one of the early inductees into the Hockey Hall of Fame, into which Boucher followed him.

Despite his three goals, as soon as Frank Nighbor returned from his injury Boucher was back in the dressing room playing cards with the other substitutes. Boucher estimated that in his season with the Senators he probably only played about one hour of hockey in total. Although this meant that he earned $1,200 to play one hour, it was not the type of career that he wanted.

After a year in Ottawa, Boucher signed a contract to play for Frank Patrick's Vancouver Maroons in the Western Hockey League, where he made the All Star Team the first three seasons he played with the Maroons.

Around this time he received the nickname Raffles. Legend has it that a local sportswriter named him Raffles after a fictional safecracker who was the central character in a book called *The Amateur Cracksman* written by E. R. Hornung, the brother-in-law of Sir Arthur Conan Doyle. In the book, Raffles was "a gentleman safecracker." This moniker was in tribute to Boucher's ability to steal the puck away from opposition players and yet play the game in a most gentlemanly manner.

Boucher remained on the west coast, skating with the Maroons for four seasons. He was named to the All Star Team in 1923, 1924, and 1925. Boucher led the Maroons in assists during the 1924–1925 season. When the league folded he was sold to the Boston Bruins. But before the season started, Conn Smythe, who was helping the Rangers put together their first NHL roster, purchased Boucher's contract for $15,000.

Later in life Boucher recalled a humorous incident surrounding Conn Smythe's acquisition of Boucher for the Rangers. Smythe had been hired by the ownership of the new franchise that was about to begin operating as the New York Rangers. It seems that when Smythe was putting the team together he first acquired the Cook brothers from the Saskatoon Crescents of the Western Canadian Hockey League. Both Bill and Frederick "Bun" Cook had been all-stars in the Western Hockey League.

Smythe, perhaps because he had great respect for their hockey knowledge and abilities, asked the Cooks whom they would like to have as the centre on their line. They said they would like Frank Boucher.

This was a dramatic time in Boucher's life. His wife had almost died giving birth to their first child. The stress of almost losing his wife and then taking care of their home while she convalesced took its toll on him.

Consequently when Smythe went to meet Boucher for the first time he was in for a surprise. Boucher, the man that the Cook brothers wanted to centre their line, looked nothing like a premier hockey player. He was pale and gaunt, weighing only 134 pounds. Conn Smythe took one look at him and said, "You're Boucher? You're the man I paid $15,000 for? You're the Cooks' choice?" With that, Frank said, Smythe walked away, sadly shaking his head.

Before the Rangers' first season began, Smythe was fired. The new man at the helm of the New York club was Lester Patrick, who contacted Boucher and told him he was going to create a line with Boucher centring Bill and Bun Cook. Ultimately, this line stayed together for a decade and during that time they innovated new ways of playing the game, such as passing patterns and set plays.

The Cook-Boucher-Cook line proved so effective that

the Rangers captured the Stanley Cup in the 1927–1928 season — only their second year in the National Hockey League. This troika would again lead the Rangers to the Stanley Cup in the 1932–1933 season. They were given the unique moniker, the "A" Line, because the subway line that ran under Madison Square Garden was called the "A" Train.

After Boucher's first season with the Rangers in the National Hockey League, a new rule was instituted because of his ability to hook and poke check the puck away from opposing players. To be more effective at these checks, Boucher spliced an extra piece of wood, 10 or 11 inches long (25.4 or 27.9 cm), onto the end of his stick. But, the league decided that this was too much of an advantage for the skilled checker. Consequently, the National Hockey League implemented a rule that limited the length of a hockey stick to 53 inches (134.6 cm). This was 10 inches (25.4 cm) shorter than the length of Boucher's stick.

During his career with the Rangers he won the Lady Byng Trophy, given for sportsmanship and gentlemanly conduct combined with performance in play, an incredible seven times (1928, 1929, 1930, 1931, 1933, 1934, and 1935). This mark so impressed the NHL that after Boucher's seventh Byng Trophy nomination he was given permanent possession of the trophy. The league continued to hand out the award, but after 1935 the recipients were given a different trophy.

Boucher was more than a gentlemanly player. He was able to combine skilful playmaking with points accumulation.

In three of the seasons that he was awarded the Byng Trophy, 1928–1929, 1929–1930, and 1932–1933, he also led the league in assists.

Although Boucher's professional-hockey-playing brothers were rough and ready players, he had chosen to play hockey in a less boisterous manner. Boucher had grown up idolizing Frank Nighbor, the great centre for his hometown Ottawa Senators. Nighbor was a skilled player who seldom, if ever, lost his temper. Instead of bodychecking his opponents, Nighbor developed the techniques of the hook check and the poke check to relieve his opponents of the puck. As a youngster, Frank Boucher practised very hard to emulate his hero.

Although he was known for his gentlemanly play, Boucher did have one fight during his NHL career. It occurred during his first game as a New York Ranger. New York was in its first NHL season and it was their first game against the Montreal Maroons. The Montreal team was big, fast, and rough. Throughout the game they had been doing their best to intimidate the Rangers.

When New York got the lead they began to retaliate against the Maroons in response to their rough play. Throughout the game Merlyn "Bad" Bill Phillips of the Maroons had been making Boucher's life miserable. When a brawl began, the usually mild-mannered Boucher decided to square the score with his opponent.

Arthur Daley of the *New York Times* described it this way: "Being a gentleman, Frank dropped his stick, peeled off his gloves and smacked "Bad" Bill on the whiskers. The polite Boucher helped his stricken foe to his feet and knocked him down again. Politely he returned Phillips to the vertical once more, only to have that unappreciative citizen conk him on the noggin with his hockey stick. End of fight."

The New York Rangers entered the final round of the 1927–1928 playoffs as definite underdogs. They were facing the defending Stanley Cup champions, the Montreal Maroons. As expected the Maroons came out roaring in the first game and won by a score of 2–0.

If the Maroons were expecting the series to be easy, the second game dispelled these thoughts as the two teams battled to a 1–1 tie after three periods of regulation play. But the second game is also well-known in NHL history for another reason. During that game, Lorne Chabot, the Rangers goaltender, was injured. In this era, teams carried only one goalie. When a goaltender was injured both teams agreed upon a neutral backup. However, when Chabot was hurt, the Maroons would not allow the Rangers to use either Alex Connell of the Senators or minor leaguer Hughie McCormick, both of whom were in the stands at the game. Coach Lester Patrick met with Bun Cook and Boucher to discuss the situation. Out of this conversation, it was decided that the coach, Lester Patrick, would play goal. Patrick allowed only one goal, and the game ended in a tie. In overtime, Montreal was stunned by a Boucher goal that gave the Rangers the win and tied the series at a game apiece. But, the outcome of the game was almost anti-climatic compared to the goaltending feat of the silver-haired coach.

Game three was a repeat of game one, with the Maroons winning 2–0. In the fourth game of this best-of-five series, the Rangers were facing elimination. But stellar goaltending and another timely goal from Boucher led the Rangers back from the brink of disaster to a 1–0 victory.

In game five, with the Maroons up by a score of 1–0, the situation did not look good for the Rangers when they were called for a penalty. Boucher was sent out to kill the penalty. But Frank had other ideas. Instead of ragging the puck to kill the penalty, he took the puck and headed toward the Maroons' end of the rink. The Montreal player defending against him was none other than Mervyn "Red" Dutton, an all-star performer in his own right. Decades later, Boucher recalled the incident:

"I knew his weakness," said Boucher. "If you pushed the puck through his legs, instead of watching you he'd look down at the puck. I tried the trick and sure enough, he looked down. By the time he looked up I was around him. I picked up the puck, skated in on Clint Benedict, Montreal's goalie, and flipped it into the right corner."

The score was tied.

But the Rangers could not help but flirt with disaster. They were called for another penalty and once again Boucher was sent out to kill it. He took the puck to centre ice. As he headed down the ice he tried a trick play to get around a Montreal defender. Frank attempted to pass the puck to himself by shooting the puck off the boards and picking up the carom. But he misjudged the angle and the puck bounced down the ice away from him. The puck was in an area of the ice approximately the same distance from the Montreal defender, Dunc Munro, as it was from Boucher. Frank recalled what happened next:

"I was watching him," said Boucher. "He skated for it. Then, I could almost hear him think, 'By God, I can't get there in time.' He seemed to stop in one motion and then he changed his mind and went for the puck. By this time I was there. I just swooped over to one side, let him go by and then I had the whole ice to myself."

Boucher fired the puck past Benedict, and the Rangers had won their first Stanley Cup. Frank Boucher had played a significant part in helping his team capture the league championship as he scored all three game winning goals.

The Rangers once again challenged for the Stanley Cup in 1933, this time against the Toronto Maple Leafs. The man behind the Leafs' bench was none other than Conn Smythe, the person who had played such a large role in assembling the Rangers' team.

Boucher retired at the end of the 1937–1938 season, his 12th season with the Rangers. It marked the end of an outstanding NHL playing career. Boucher had been selected to the Second All Star Team in 1931. Two years later he began a stretch of three seasons, 1933, 1934, and 1935, in which he was named the centre of the NHL's First All Star Team.

After hanging up his skates, Boucher became the coach of the New York Rovers, the Rangers' Eastern United States Amateur Hockey League farm club. He later was promoted by the organization to become the coach and general manager of the Rangers.

While Boucher was coaching the Rangers he implemented the idea of pulling the goalie while play was going on. It was the middle of the 1939–1940 season. Boucher recalled that the Rangers had won something like 18 games in a row. They were in Chicago, and despite outplaying the Blackhawks they were losing 1–0. At the end of the second period, Boucher told Rangers' goalie Dave Kerr that if they were behind near the end of the third period, he would signal for him to rush to the bench and hopefully the surprise of six attackers would lead to a Ranger goal.

Near the end of the game, Boucher signalled his goalie to come to the bench. When Ranger general manager Lester Patrick saw Ott Heller jump over the boards and join in the play, he was sure that his club had too many men on the ice. He raced to the Ranger bench yelling at Boucher that they had too many men on the ice. The Chicago coach heard Patrick and shouted to the referee that New York had too many men on the ice. The referee blew the whistle, but before he could hand out a penalty for too many men on the ice, he realized the Rangers didn't have too many men on the ice — because they had no goalie in their net! The Rangers' surprise attack was uncovered.

The Blackhawks managed to win the game and end the

Rangers' winning streak. But the most embarrassed person in the arena was Lester Patrick.

Boucher was also a member of the National Hockey League's Rule Committee and later the head of junior hockey in Saskatchewan. Ironically, Boucher was a member of the Rules Committee that instituted the red line in the 1940s. He explained that the reason for the inception of this rule was that, because teams could only pass to their own blueline, the defensive team was sometimes bottled up for five minutes at a time. The red line was brought about to increase the length of passes and create a more even flow of play. In 1962, Boucher felt that the red line should be removed once again to stop the overly defensive style of play that was invading the National Hockey League. He argued, "forward passing should be allowed to the opposing team's blueline." Boucher reasoned that if the defensive team could fire the puck that far out of their own end, defencemen could no longer "pinch in" effectively in the offensive zone because they could get caught out of position. He also stated that removing the red line would allow for a more even flow to play. More than four decades later, the NHL took Boucher's advice and the red line was removed from play in the 2005–2006 season.

In 1958 Boucher's contributions to hockey were recognized when he was inducted into the Hockey Hall of Fame. And in 1993, Frank Boucher was awarded the prestigious Lester Patrick Award for his contributions to furthering the sport of hockey in the United States.

Chapter 6
Alex Delvecchio: A Quiet and Classy Guy

Durability must have been Alex Delvecchio's middle name. Although his career spanned 22 National Hockey League seasons, he missed only 43 games.

Delvecchio might also be the "Rodney Dangerfield" of the National Hockey League. (He never seems to get the respect due a player who amassed 1,281 career points.) When he retired in 1973, Delvecchio was second only to Gordie Howe in total points. Even his nickname, "Fats," is hardly respectful of a smooth-skating and brilliantly passing player who has climbed his way to the upper echelons of longevity and points accumulation in the National Hockey League.

Peter Alexander "Fats" Delvecchio was born on

Alex Delvecchio: A Quiet and Classy Guy

December 4, 1931, in Fort William (now known as Thunder Bay), Ontario. His nickname engenders visions that are less than complimentary for an athlete. However, according to Jack Berry of *The Detroit Free Press*, Delvecchio was called "Fats" because of his round, full face.

Delvecchio played hockey up to midget ranks before joining the Fort William Hurricanes junior team. It was while he was playing for the Hurricanes that Lou Passador, a Red Wings' scout who also coached a junior club in the area, informed the Wings of the vast potential of the young Delvecchio.

At the age of 18, the already six-foot-tall, 175-pound youngster found himself headed to southern Ontario to play for the Red Wings' junior farm club, the Oshawa Generals. Even as a junior his playmaking abilities were outstanding and an indication of his future greatness was illustrated to the hockey world when he scored 49 goals and an amazing 72 assists during his 1950–1951 season with the Generals. This astounding total was probably the reason why he was given a one-game trial with the Red Wings that same year.

Delvecchio started the next season with the Wings' farm club in Indianapolis, and after six games he had netted three goals and six assists. At this point, Red Wings' general manager Jack Adams felt Delvecchio was ready for the NHL. Once he arrived in Detroit he played on a line with Metro Prystai and Johnny Wilson on his wings.

Delvecchio joined a team that was laden with stars such as Red Kelly, Sid Abel, Ted Lindsay, and, perhaps the greatest player of all time, Gordie Howe. Despite being a rookie on such a star-studded veteran team, Delvecchio did not demonstrate any awkwardness about his new surroundings. He started his NHL career in style. In his second game, the Wings faced the Toronto Maple Leafs. When these two clubs clashed the action was intense, but the rookie was not over-awed to be facing-off against future Hall of Fame centres Teeder Kennedy or Max Bentley. Delvecchio set up both Detroit goals in a 2–2 tie.

His first four goals were dramatic. Delvecchio scored twice and assisted on a third to erase a 4–1 New York Ranger lead and earn a tie for the Red Wings. His fourth goal marked another three-goal comeback that resulted in a tie with Montreal.

In another game against the Canadiens, Delvecchio once again proved to his teammates and the rest of the league that the star-power of opposition teams did not intimidate him. The Canadiens line-up featured stars on every line, yet the young Delvecchio, with his team desperately needing goals, picked up the puck in his own end and wove his way through the entire Montreal team. He circled the net and, before another Canadiens' defender could challenge him, the rookie fired the puck behind a surprised Gerry McNeil into the Montreal net. Moments later, he intercepted a clearing pass by a Montreal defender. Before the Canadiens could recover he laid a perfect pass on the stick of Marcel Pronovost, who quickly scored to tie the game. All four goals were important to saving his team from defeat. Delvecchio proved from the very beginning that he could always be counted on to score or set up important goals for his team.

In his first 20 games in the National Hockey League Delvecchio scored four goals and seven assists, and by the end of his inaugural season he had notched 15 goals as the Red Wings captured the Stanley Cup.

The next season, star centre Sid Abel left Detroit to become the player/coach of the Chicago Blackhawks, spelling the end of the Red Wings' famous Production Line. But the reality of the situation was that it only marked the beginning of a new version of that highly effective line. During the 1952–1953 season, the smooth-skating Delvecchio joined Howe and the pugnacious Ted Lindsay on Detroit's top line. Delvecchio quickly proved that he belonged there, being named to the league's Second All Star Team the first season that he played with Howe and Lindsay. Although Lindsay remained only a few more seasons in Detroit, Howe and Delvecchio played together as linemates for almost two decades. During the late 1950s and most of the 1960s a number of left wingers skated with the dynamic duo. Despite what must have often seemed to be a revolving door on their left flank, Howe and Delvecchio amassed scoring totals that were considered virtually unattainable by mere mortals, until the coming of the Gretzky era.

Consequently, the two shared a lot of career milestones. On October 30, 1970, Delvecchio stole the puck from superstar

Bobby Orr and scored his 400th career goal. Later in the same game he scored again, off an assist that marked Howe's 1,000th career assist. Delvecchio also assisted on Howe's 700th career goal, while another Howe marker, on February 21, 1971, was set up by Delvecchio's 1,000th career point. Delvecchio was only the third NHL player to reach this milestone.

Delvecchio was not only durable, but versatile. He was named the centre on the Second All Star Team in 1953 and six years later, in 1959, was selected as the left winger on the Second All Star Team. This feat made Delvecchio only the third player in the history of the National Hockey League, after Dit Clapper and former teammate Sid Abel, to achieve All Star Team honours in the NHL at two different positions.

In game seven of the 1954–1955 Stanley Cup finals, Detroit defeated the Canadiens 3–1 with Delvecchio scoring two goals to clinch the Cup for the Red Wings. The entire series had featured his hockey prowess, as he scored seven goals and eight assists.

During the 1956–1957 season he suffered an ankle injury that kept him out of the line-up for 22 games. Remarkably, Delvecchio only missed 21 other games during his entire career!

Throughout his career he was consistently a 20-goals-per-season scorer. It is important to remember that although a 20-goal season is commonplace today, in the 1950s and 1960s only a few stars reached this plateau each year.

Delvecchio was a gentleman on and off the ice. On three

Alex Delvecchio

occasions he was awarded the Lady Byng Memorial Trophy (1959, 1966, and 1969). In a 1970 *Hockey Illustrated* interview he talked about winning this award. Delvecchio revealed that he'd once rued winning the Byng trophies, because general manager Jack Adams had almost traded him after he'd won his first Byng Trophy. Adams thought it indicated that Delvecchio lacked fire and determination. Adams' negative attitude toward

Byng recipients had already been illustrated in the late 1940s; when star defenceman Bill Quackenbush won the Byng, it was not long before Adams traded him to another team. Delvecchio said, "I wish they wouldn't call that trophy the *Lady* Byng. Maybe it should be the Lord Byng or something."

During the 1962–1963 season, coach Sid Abel named Delvecchio to wear the "C" on his jersey, replacing Howe. Abel selected Howe and veteran defenceman Bill Gadsby to act as Delvecchio's assistant captains. Many questioned Abel's motives for stripping the "C" from Howe's jersey. The answer, according to the Red Wings' coach, was simple. The captain of a team has to be comfortable speaking out in the dressing room, with game officials, and performing community service functions, such as public speaking. Delvecchio was not only known for his fun-loving approach to life and general affability, but also, like Howe, had the respect of his teammates and others throughout the world of hockey. Whatever the reason, Delvecchio thrived as the captain, and his 12-season captaincy of the Red Wings was a club record until current captain Steve Yzerman surpassed it.

In a March 1970 article in *Hockey Illustrated,* Delvecchio's long-time right winger, the incomparable Gordie Howe, complained, "I don't like to play on the same line as Fats. He is such a smooth skater with that almost delicate toe dancing style of his that he is worth watching. I can only watch him when he is playing on a different line ..."

In the 1965–1966 playoffs Delvecchio tried his best

to lead his team to another Stanley Cup, leading all playoff scorers that year with 11 assists. But, unfortunately for the Red Wings, Henri Richard scored a goal, which is still disputed by Detroit's long-time fans, to capture the Cup for the Montreal Canadiens. When one considers the injuries to key Red Wings' players, it's surprising they were able to take the series to six games. The defence corps was badly beaten up. Bill Gadsby played despite broken blood vessels in his elbow and a broken toe. Gary Bergman had a torn calf muscle. Bert Marshall played the last two games of the series with a severe charley horse. Norm Ullman played with a badly bruised chest. Goaltender Roger Crozier, who won the Conn Smythe Trophy as the series MVP, tended net brilliantly despite the fact that he played the last two games with a twisted knee. With all Delvecchio's walking wounded trying to capture the Cup, their captain tried to carry a bigger share of the load, but even his scoring feats were not enough.

The 1968–1969 season saw Delvecchio centring a modern version of the Production Line as Frank Mahovlich joined him and Howe on the Wings' number one line. The results were historic! They set a record, scoring 118 goals in a season by one line while amassing 254 points. These totals are spectacular when you consider that the combined age of the line was 110 years, and that the threesome had 57 years of playing experience.

Because Delvecchio scored only 25 goals during the record season and Mahovlich and Howe scored 49 and 44 goals respectively, he received few of the accolades for the record. Delvecchio's contributions to the line's productivity were almost totally ignored as his two high profile wingers got most of the recognition. But some hockey writers of that era pointed out that when Red Wings' coach Bill Gadsby split up the trio and inserted rising NHL star Gary Unger with the two superstar wingers, the line was ineffective.

Despite the scoring feats of the Howe, Mahovlich, and Delvecchio version of the Production Line, Delvecchio experienced a 31-game streak where he failed to score a goal. Although the line continued to pile up the points, his scoring drought came to the attention of hockey fans. Delvecchio received lucky pins, broaches, and other good luck omens to help him pot a goal. He tried smearing his hockey stick blade with tobacco juice. Nothing helped. Someone gave him a sprig of white heather from Scotland, which he mistakenly called English holly. He put it in his skate boot for luck. Unfortunately, all it did was tickle his foot when he put his skates on.

Finally, Delvecchio's luck changed, but not without some controversy. Detroit was playing the Boston Bruins. Frank Mahovlich attempted a pass to Delvecchio who was in front of the net. Somehow, the puck eluded his stick and bounced into the net off of his body. Eddie Johnston, the Bruins' goalie, chased referee Art Skov all the way to centre ice protesting that Fats had kicked the puck into the net. Johnston yelled at Skov, "I don't care if he goes 62 games without a goal, that one shouldn't count." But, as always, the referee is right. The goal counted and Delvecchio's scoring drought was over.

In 1973–1974 Delvecchio retired to become the coach of the Red Wings. When he hung up his skates for the last time he was second only to Gordie Howe in games played, and assists and total points accumulated over his career. Delvecchio was also only the second player, again behind Howe, to play more than 20 seasons with the same NHL club.

In 1974, he was honoured with the Lester Patrick Trophy for his outstanding service to the sport of hockey in the United States. In 1977, Delvecchio was elected to the Hockey Hall of Fame.

On November 10, 1991, the Red Wings honoured Alex Delvecchio by raising his #10 jersey to the rafters of the Joe Louis Arena.

Alex Delvecchio is perhaps the forgotten man of National Hockey League history. But his numbers rank with the best of his era. It has often been suggested that his problem was that he was too quiet a player. He never used his 200-pound body to pummel the opposition into submission, choosing instead to finesse his way around his opponents. His point totals suggest he was more than successful using this style of play. But perhaps the biggest obstacles to having Delvecchio receive the accolades he so richly deserved were his teammates. Throughout his career he was surrounded by legends. Terry Sawchuk, Red Kelly, Ted Lindsay, Frank Mahovlich, and, of course, his famous right winger Gordie Howe all demanded a lot of ink from hockey writers and a lot of attention from fans. When it was all said and done there seemed to be little time or recognition for the smooth-skating, adept-passing, mild-mannered Alex Delvecchio.

Chicago's all-star goalie, Tony Esposito, said in an interview in the April 1972 edition of *Hockey Magazine*, "Calling Alex underrated … is deceptive because he's played next to Howe. But he's a very effective forward and always in the right position. You can't give him too much room or he'll kill you."

Chapter 7

Theodore S. "Teeder" Kennedy: "Come oonnn, Teeder!"

Had it not been for a quirk of fate, this legendary Maple Leaf might have ended up wearing the red, white, and blue of Toronto's most hated foe, the Montreal Canadiens.

Theodore S. "Teeder" Kennedy was born on December 12, 1925, in Humberstone, Ontario, which today is a part of the city of Port Colborne. How Kennedy became known as Teeder is not quite clear. In a *Legends of Hockey* article, Kennedy related that his Christian name was Theodore and that as a child this had proved to be a difficult name for his young friends to say, and somehow they mispronounced it as Teeder. Whatever the origin, his moniker is a part of Maple Leaf legend.

At the age of 16, the Montreal Canadiens signed Kennedy to a contract. But, when he attended his first training camp with the Canadiens Kennedy became so homesick that he packed up his gear and left training camp abruptly.

Back home in Port Colborne he played amateur hockey with a local club. It was here that he came to the attention of former National Hockey League scoring great, Nels Stewart, who was coaching the Port Colborne senior team. Stewart was to have a deep impact on the young player. Kennedy recalled, "Nels taught me how to operate in front of the net ... something basic — take a long look before you shoot the puck. Don't rush. Coming from Nels, I never forgot the lessons." He learned quickly from Stewart as, during his season under his tutelage with Port Colborne Sailors, Kennedy scored 23 goals in 23 games and added an impressive 29 assists.

Leafs fans should never forget to be thankful to Stewart for bringing them a great player to wear their beloved blue and white jersey. Recognizing a potentially great hockey player, Stewart told Frank Selke, then-acting general manager of the Maple Leafs, of Kennedy's capabilities. Perhaps respecting Stewart's hockey knowledge, Selke acted upon it, arranging a trade with Montreal. This transaction was to have an impact on the Leafs, both on and off the ice. Not only would they acquire one of their greatest performers of all time, but the trade would ultimately create a dramatic transformation of the Maple Leafs' front office and, later, the Montreal management team.

Conn Smythe, legendary owner of the Maple Leafs, provided some interesting insight into the Eddols-for-Kennedy trade in his memoirs, *Conn Smythe: If You Can't Beat 'Em in the Alley.* Smythe recalled, "I was furious about not even being consulted. Eddols had joined the Air Force soon after signing with us, and I thought trading him was a stinking trick to play on a man who was going overseas." Smythe's attitude toward the trading of Eddols is understandable, because he was very loyal to players who gave up the game to enlist during the war.

Frank Selke acted as general manager of the Leafs while Smythe himself was overseas with the Canadian armed forces during World War II. Selke suspected his relationship with Smythe ran into trouble because he had failed to notify the owner of the impending trade.

Smythe said that he would probably have agreed to the trade because his age made Kennedy exempt from military duty and the Leafs had been hard hit by the fact that so many of their veterans had been called to duty.

When Smythe returned from the war, his relationship with Selke cooled. Some suggest that Smythe feared the Kennedy trade signalled the beginning of a power shift in the Leafs' management offices, and that ultimately he would find himself "on the outside, looking in" at Selke and others running the team *he* had built. So Smythe made things difficult for Selke, who ultimately moved on to Montreal. There, he made a significant contribution to creating the Canadiens' teams that would dominate the National Hockey League for many years.

Teeder began playing for the Leafs at the age of 18. During his 12-season career with Toronto he played on five Stanley Cup championship teams. Kennedy was known for his hard work and dedication to his team and to the sport of hockey, so it was no surprise that he was awarded the Hart Trophy as the MVP in 1954–1955, his last professional hockey campaign.

Conn Smythe said that he could have watched Kennedy play forever because he worked so hard.

One of the few knocks against Kennedy was that he was not considered to be a very good skater. Teammate Howie Meeker described him as "a thoroughbred plough horse." Conn Smythe provided an interesting perspective on this point in his memoirs. "Al Nickleson then was working for the *The Globe*. Every time Kennedy carried the puck Nickleson would write about how he laboured up the ice, etc., etc. Oh the pity of it all, that kind of crap. Sure he laboured. That was his style. But I never saw anybody catch him when he had the puck, and that's what counts."

He may not have been the best skater, but Smythe was right. Kennedy was known throughout the league as one of the best defensive centres in the game as well as perhaps the premier face-off man in the business.

And he was popular with Leafs fans at Maple Leaf Gardens. A long-time season ticket holder and ardent Maple Leaf fan, John Arnott, could often be heard at Leafs games.

Arnott's voice boomed above the rest of throng, exhorting his favourite Leaf to lead them to victory. Bill Barilko's sister, Anne, remembered travelling from Timmins to Toronto to watch her brother play and hearing Arnott shout, "Come onnnnnn, Teeeeder!" In Kevin Shea's book about her brother, *Barilko: Without a Trace*, she recalled, "hearing that [Arnott's cheer] at a game was very exciting." Fan enthusiasm such as this added, without doubt, to the Kennedy legend.

The 1943–1944 season was Kennedy's first full campaign with the Toronto Maple Leafs. In his second season his scoring prowess came to the fore as he led the club to a surprise Stanley Cup victory over the Canadiens. Kennedy was the goal-scoring leader in that successful playoff run. In 1946, Kennedy was teamed with Howie Meeker and Vic Lynn on a line that was dubbed the Kid Line ll in honour of the great Maple Leafs' Kid Line of Primeau, Jackson, and Connacher that dominated the NHL in the mid-1930s. Later Kennedy's line was renamed the KLM Line. No matter what its moniker, this line led the Maple Leafs to three successive Stanley Cup victories in 1947, 1948, and 1949. This combination of players certainly seemed to benefit Kennedy, who led the team in scoring with 28 goals and 32 assists. Those 60 points placed him fifth in the league's scoring race (behind scoring champion Max Bentley who would later become his teammate).

The 1946–1947 Stanley Cup finals started badly for the Leafs as the Canadiens thoroughly demolished them with a

6–0 victory. But the second game saw Toronto tie the series, largely due to the efforts of the KLM Line.

In the first minute of play, the Leafs, led by Kennedy, rushed the Montreal net and at 1:12 of the opening period Teeder fired the puck into the net. And just in case the Canadiens hadn't received the message that Toronto was not about to roll over and play dead for them, less than half a minute after his goal, Kennedy fed a pass to his linemate Vic Lyn who promptly deposited the puck into the back of the Montreal net. The Canadiens had been warned!

The early 2–0 lead unsettled the Canadiens, whose play became very chippy. As the rough play escalated, things only got better for Toronto. Perhaps the biggest break occurred when Montreal's volatile superstar, Rocket Richard, slashed Vic Lyn in the head, cutting him severely over the eye and knocking him unconscious. Later in the game Richard once again attacked a Leaf player with a vicious slash to the head. This assault on Bill Ezinicki earned the Canadiens' star a one game suspension. Without the Rocket, the Canadiens lost game three.

The fourth game was as violent as the others, but a closer scoring affair that was finally settled when Apps put one in the net to give the Leafs an overtime victory.

After the Canadiens claimed victory on home ice in game five, the teams returned to Toronto where, fittingly, scoring leader Teeder Kennedy drilled home the game-winning and series-ending goal. Once again, Toronto had won the Stanley Cup.

Syl Apps, Ted Kennedy, and George Armstrong

In 1947–1948, perhaps inspired by their Stanley Cup victory the previous year, the Leafs finished first in the standings and opened their Cup defence in a semifinal series against the Boston Bruins. After winning the series opener, the Leafs looked to grab a stranglehold on the series with another home ice victory in the second game. Once again, Kennedy led the way with a hat trick in the 5–3 Toronto victory. The tone of the series had been set. The Leafs disposed of the Bruins in five games and then prepared to meet the Red Wings in the Cup final.

Despite Detroit's best efforts, the Leafs were too much for them. Led by playoff scoring leader Teeder Kennedy, Toronto captured the Stanley Cup in four games.

Syl Apps retired at the end of the 1948 season and Kennedy was named to replace him as captain. Conn Smythe suggested that although the loss of Apps was hard on the club, it may have been even tougher on Kennedy. The Leafs' owner always felt that after Apps left the team, Kennedy tried too hard to fill the void created by the former captain's departure. But even if there was some basis for Smythe's concerns, Kennedy continued to be a stellar performer for many more years.

If there was a low point in Teeder Kennedy's career, it probably occurred in the first game of the 1949–1950 playoff series against the Detroit Red Wings. At 8:41 of the third period, Gordie Howe attempted to check Kennedy and instead crashed into the boards. The Red Wings' star, near death, lay crumpled on the ice. He had suffered a fractured skull, a broken nose, a broken collarbone, and a scratched eye. Seeing their teammate lying on the ice in a pool of blood, the incensed Red Wings attacked Kennedy. Soon players from both teams were battling on the ice. Leafs' coach Hap Day managed to get Kennedy off the ice, but the rough play continued. Even after the game, Detroit players vowed to "get Kennedy" for what they described as his vicious attack by the Leaf player on Howe.

With the passage of time cooler heads prevailed and the Red Wings relaxed their attempts to exact retribution on Teeder. In the February 1969 edition of *Hockey Illustrated*, Sid Abel recalled the incident. "It was kind of a chippy game that night," recalled Abel. "Everybody was taking a run at one another. I thought Gordie got a butt end. Later I felt sorry for Kennedy. He got the brunt of it from all angles — players *and* fans."

In a 1975 interview with author Jack Batten, Teeder recalled the incident from his perspective. The referee, George Gravel, had his hand up to signal a charging penalty to Howe, when the Detroit star missed Kennedy and crashed into the boards. He claimed that everybody saw this, including Clarence Campbell, who "was sitting right there and saw everything, the president of the league."

Kennedy went on to explain why, despite all this evidence, the Detroit players and fans continued to blame him for Howe's injuries. He claimed that Red Wings' general manager, Jack Adams, "was from the old school of letting your emotions run away, and stirred up a fuss, blaming me for Howe's injury." Everybody listened to these accusations because, "James Norris Sr., the old man, was still alive then. He was very influential. He owned the Red Wings, owned most of Chicago, and had some ownership of Madison Square Garden, so when he made waves, you felt water all over the league. At any rate, the guys on our team were very upset over the criticism of me. It took a lot of starch out of us."

Perhaps it was the injury to Howe that inspired the Red

Wings or it was intimidation exacted upon Kennedy and the other Leafs, or a combination of both. But the Wings defeated the Leafs in the semifinal, ending Toronto's three-season Stanley Cup winning streak. Detroit then went on to capture the Stanley Cup "for their injured teammate."

And, of course, it was Teeder who made a key play to set up Bill Barilko's overtime goal in the 1950–1951 Stanley Cup playoffs. Barilko was the most unlikely of hockey scoring heroes, and his goal is forever cemented in the memories of NHL fans by the fact that he disappeared that same summer while on a fishing expedition in the northern Ontario barrens. Had it not been for a key play by Teeder Kennedy, Barilko might never have scored that famous goal.

In August 1951 J. P. Bickell, one of Conn Smythe's longtime business associates, passed away. Bickell had been a key contributor to the quick and efficient building of Maple Leaf Gardens during the depression years, and also an important member of the Maple Leafs' management team. To honour this great hockey entrepreneur the Maple Leafs established a trophy in his name. The Bickell Trophy recognizes great contributions to the Toronto Maple Leafs hockey club. This trophy is not an annual award. Instead, it can be given out at the discretion of the Board of Directors — for one tremendous feat, for a season of spectacular play, or for remarkable long-term service. The first player to be so recognized, and the trophy's first recipient, was Teeder Kennedy in 1953. Only a select few in the long and storied history of the Toronto

Maple Leafs have been honoured to join Kennedy as Bickell Trophy recipients. They include Harry Lumley, Tod Sloan, George Armstrong, Bob Pulford, Johnny Bower, Red Kelly, Dave Keon, Allan Stanley, Terry Sawchuk, Tim Horton, Bob Baun, King Clancy, Mike Palmateer, Bob Davidson, Doug Gilmour, Mats Sundin, Curtis Joseph, and Pat Quinn.

Teeder Kennedy holds the Maple Leafs record for most points in the Stanley Cup finals with 23. George Armstrong and Frank Mahovlich are next with 22 each, followed by Syl Apps and Bob Pulford with 21 each.

In 1966 Teeder Kennedy was inducted into the Hockey Hall of Fame. This was the same year that his teammate Max Bentley was named to the Hall of Fame. And on October 3, 1993, the Toronto Maple Leafs once again recognized the phenomenal contributions of Teeder Kennedy when they hoisted a banner bearing his image and his #9 jersey to the rafters of Maple Leaf Gardens.

Chapter 8
Henri Richard:
The Pocket Rocket

Despite spending his entire hockey career in the shadow of his superstar older brother, Maurice "Rocket" Richard, Henri "the Pocket Rocket" Richard became one of the most decorated hockey players of all time. Henri may have lacked the size, strength, and dark reputation of his older brother, but he won more Stanley Cups. With 11 Stanley Cups, he leads both the Montreal Canadiens and the National Hockey League.

Henri Richard is probably the only player to celebrate his fifth birthday while playing in the National Hockey League! But Richard wasn't a childhood phenomena — just a leap year baby. Henri was born on February 29, 1936.

Henri Richard had been a good hockey player, starring in the junior ranks in the Montreal area. Nonetheless, his older brother, Maurice, who was 33 years old, was ecstatic about the possibility of playing with the young Henri.

Henri's short stature was always the first thing coaches and scouts noticed. When he was 12 years old, Maurice asked Pete Morin, a Canadiens' scout, to have a look at his kid brother. Morin discovered a youngster who could skate like the wind but who only weighed 125 pounds.

Despite his short stature and slight build, when he was 12 years old Richard played Junior "B" with players who were as old as 19. Two years later, at the age of 14 he was playing Junior "A" hockey. In 1953–1954, he skated with the Montreal Junior Canadiens. Henri scored 56 goals in 54 games and accumulated 109 points. The following season, his last as a junior, Henri notched 33 goals and 33 assists in 44 games.

The next season, the 19-year-old younger Richard once again came to the Canadiens' training camp. But when he showed up, all the talk was about his short stature. Sceptics felt that, at only 5'7", the youngster would never last in the NHL. But in his memoirs, Boom Boom Geoffrion stated Henri was "a good skater and stickhandler and, most important, he wasn't afraid of anything."

Whereas Maurice would usually power his way around (or just as often as not, through) an opposing player, Henri was a tireless skater. He would use effortless strides to weave across and up and down the ice to outmanoeuvre his opponents, and then with a sudden burst of speed he would zoom toward the net. General Manager Frank Selke once said that Richard was an extremely fast skater, but what really separated him from the other speedsters in the game was that Richard could maintain his high speed while he carried the puck.

At training camp there were always comparisons made between Henri and his older brother, but one day the brothers provided a nervous moment for their teammates and the club's management. It was during a scrimmage and both brothers were in full flight coming from opposite ends of the ice. Everything came to an abrupt halt when the Rocket zigged and the Pocket zagged. The collision sent shock waves through the Forum. Frank Selke recalled, in *Lions in Winter*, that when the Rocket awoke in the trainer's room, Henri was standing anxiously over him. He looked sternly up at his little brother and said, "Henri, you gotta watch out. You could get hurt out there."

When Henri met with Frank Selke to sign his first contract, it was Maurice who acted as his agent. Interestingly, the older brother also acted as his interpreter, since Henri spoke very little English.

They agreed upon a $7,000 salary with a $2,000 signing bonus. But, as they were leaving the office, Selke called them back and ripped up the contract and replaced it with one that gave Henri a $5,000 signing bonus. Selke said later that he changed the contract because he did not want Henri to think later that he had taken advantage of the youngster.

Despite the many "experts" who said that the younger

Richard needed more seasoning, when the season opened Coach Toe Blake pencilled him into the line-up centring his brother Maurice and Dickie Moore.

Perhaps one of the major reasons why Richard cracked the star-studded Canadiens line-up was his puck control during training camp scrimmages. In an article "Henri Richard: At the Crossroads" in the December 1967 edition of *Hockey Illustrated*, Canadiens coach Toe Blake recalled: "It got so bad, I thought of throwing out a second puck. Henri had the puck four-fifths of the time that he was on the ice."

The fact that Richard seemed glued to the puck was not unusual considering his style of play. Blake said, "He is not puck lucky ... He is smart enough to be where the puck is all the time. He is almost uncanny that way. He sizes up how a play is going to go, and then gets there, and the next thing you know he's got the puck. Sometimes, when he doesn't have things figured out in advance, he is so fast that he gets there first anyway."

The Canadiens' front office thought Richard was perfectly suited to play centre. Frank Selke described the Pocket Rocket as having "brilliant generalship" on the ice. The Canadiens' general manager went on to say that while he was not as powerful as some of the other players on the team, he possessed many other skills such as "an accurate right handed shot" and a "willingness to check even the biggest man he can single out."

During his junior career Henri had been nicknamed

Flash, but once his National Hockey League career started it was not long before someone tagged him the Pocket Rocket in reference to the size differential between him and the older, larger Rocket.

Many members of the Canadiens' front office worried that Henri's presence on the ice would create a distraction for his superstar brother. Maurice was famous (or infamous) for his volatile temper, and there was concern that he might spend more time protecting his brother and less time scoring goals. However, it quickly became apparent that Henri did not need his big brother or anyone else, for that matter, protecting him.

One of the best examples of Henri's toughness occurred on January 1, 1958, at the Boston Garden. Henri was near the top of the league in scoring and the Bruins were clearly attempting to intimidate him. They pounded him with bodychecks throughout the game. Finally, the Pocket Rocket had enough of the rough stuff.

When Boston tough guy, defenceman Fern Flaman, received a penalty Richard decided to make a statement. Ignoring the fact that his team was about to go on a power play, the Pocket Rocket launched himself into the much taller and bigger Bruin. As if possessed, he dispatched Flaman and grabbed Jack Bionda and proceeded to battle one of the league's most noted fighters. He had barely finished his trimming of Bionda when Leo Labine, another of the toughest players in the Bruins' line-up, stepped in to try his luck with the 5'7" Richard. When the dust had cleared there was a new respect in the NHL for Henri Richard. In his memoirs, Boom Boom Geoffrion quoted Boston general manager Lynn Patrick's impressions of Richard that night:

"I saw little Richard take on Fernie, Jack and Leo one right after another. Let me tell you he didn't lose a decision to any one of them. He must have fought by himself for five minutes but he didn't back up once. How he did it I don't know, but he's one heck of a fighter. You don't need any policemen to take care of him!"

When Richard came into the league he spent a lot of time fighting any and all comers in order to establish himself, and to let everyone know he did not need his big brother to protect him. After two seasons of wearing out his fists on the jaws of opponents, Richard decided to try and avoid the penalty box and spend more time on the ice. The results were amazing. His point totals jumped. After counting 40 and 54 total points respectively in his first two seasons, Richard scored 28 goals and an astonishing league high of 52 assists in his third season, and finishing second in the league scoring race with 80 points.

Richard now realized he could be far more successful and helpful to his team if he stayed away from the penalty box. From that point on, he enjoyed success as a goal scorer, often netting more than 20 goals a season.

The third period of game three in the 1960 Stanley Cup finals against the Toronto Maple Leafs marked a magic moment in the history of the National Hockey League.

The period was nearing the 11-minute mark when the Pocket Rocket headed into the Maple Leafs' zone. He saw his brother Maurice in the clear. Quickly he fired the puck to the Rocket; in the blink of an eye the puck was in the Toronto net. As the Canadiens celebrated, a few in the arena noted that the Rocket had skated over and fished the puck out of the net. This was a surprising move because the brash and volatile superstar was not known for his sentimentality.

When the Stanley Cup was once again in the possession of the Canadiens, the motive behind this move became apparent. It was to be his last NHL goal. This milestone goal, capping the career of the greatest goal scorer in the history of the game, had been set up by his brother!

Richard was a quiet-spoken player. Unless something upset him he seldom spoke out. Early in his career a reporter asked Coach Blake if Henri spoke English. Blake replied, "I don't think he even speaks French."

This reticence to speak, especially in public, became a topic of conversation when Jean Béliveau retired. There was speculation that Henri would become the captain of the Canadiens. But Richard worried about the possibility of having to make public speeches if he became the captain. In an October 1971 column, Jim Proudfoot of the *Toronto Star* quoted Richard. "I don't think I'd ever take that job if I had to make speeches in public." Richard went on to say, "I don't even like talking in private. And you know how the captain of the Canadiens speaks for the team so many times in front of big crowds. I couldn't do that. I'd have to tell them no."

But the team allayed his fears when he was told that Béliveau would continue to make the speeches for the team. As a result, Richard accepted the captaincy.

In his autobiography, Jean Béliveau described the versatility of Henri Richard. He recalled that Toronto's Norm Ullman would "leave me gasping for air. As a result, Toe Blake loved to put Henri Richard against him … If Ullman wore me out, Henri wore him out, skating with him effortlessly, bumping him off the puck in the corners or in open ice, sticking to him mercilessly, hampering his playmaking ability."

On May 5, 1966, Henri netted the Stanley Cup winning goal in a series against the Detroit Red Wings at 2:20 of overtime. His first Stanley Cup winning goal wasn't pretty … and it was surrounded in controversy.

Leon Rochefort had passed the puck to Richard, who fired it on to his other winger Dave Balon. Balon was trying to work his way toward the net, but Detroit defenceman Bert Marshall blocked the way. Richard's shot struck Marshall, then "hit" Richard and went into the net behind a startled Roger Crozier. Pandemonium broke out among the Canadiens. To put an exclamation mark on the goal, the Canadiens players rushed onto the ice, mobbing their hero and celebrating their victory.

As the Montreal players celebrated, the Red Wing goalie chased after the referee claiming that Richard had directed the puck into the net with his hand. The Canadiens argued that it had been a legal goal because it had hit Richard's knee. But all the claims and counterclaims were for naught. Referee Frank Udvari had immediately signalled a goal, and refused to hear Detroit's arguments.

To this day, long-time Detroit Red Wings fans will argue that their team was robbed of a Stanley Cup. This was especially true because of the efforts of their little goalie, Roger Crozier, who had performed beyond their wildest expectations and who, many said, really deserved a better fate than losing on a questionable call.

To add to the mystique of the goal, Canadiens' folklore suggests that Coach Toe Blake tapped Richard on the shoulder and said, "Go on out, Henri — you're going to get the winner." And 50 seconds later the Canadiens were celebrating another Stanley Cup.

In the 1970–1971 Cup finals against the Blackhawks, once again, Richard was a Stanley Cup hero. He scored the tying and winning goals in game seven, for a 3–2 Montreal victory.

Henri Richard transcended three distinct eras of Montreal Canadiens' history. When he arrived in the mid-1950s, the Canadiens were a star-studded line-up featuring his brother Maurice, Jean Béliveau, and Bernie Geoffrion. The first half of that decade had been dominated by their fierce rivalry with the Detroit Red Wings. But the latter half of the 1950s was solely the domain of the Canadiens.

By the time the 1960s arrived, many veteran Canadiens,

including Rocket Richard, had retired. Béliveau was the captain leading a new generation of Habs. The first half of the decade must have seemed like an eternal drought to the players and fans as Chicago and Toronto dominated the parade to the Stanley Cup podium.

Without Stanley Cup victories, the players of this era were being compared to the Canadiens of the past. Finally, with Henri Richard's winning goal against the Red Wings, Montreal fans and players could rest a little easier. Jean Béliveau remembered that during this era it was John Ferguson who "brought respect to the 1960s' Canadiens," but it was Henri Richard who "provided the character."

Béliveau also said that he had a lot of admiration for the younger Richard, who was always under scrutiny because of his famous older brother. No matter what he did, on or off the ice, he was compared to the Rocket. It was not until many years after Maurice retired that the comparisons diminished and people began to appreciate him as a star in his own right. But the spectre of his brother loomed over him in some regards throughout his career and beyond. Béliveau said, "All through his long career, everywhere we went, the first question anybody ever asked him was, 'How's Maurice?' Each time, he was remarkably patient. 'Maurice is fine.'" According to Béliveau, Henri Richard was "a very productive hockey player and very tough. He was also a great team player, and a great captain after I retired. It is not by chance that Henri Richard holds the all-time record of eleven Stanley Cup wins."

Perhaps an excerpt from a 1967–1968 article about the Richard brothers best sums up Henri Richard's career in terms of carrying the weight of being the younger and smaller brother of one of the greatest hockey legends of all time.

Richard had spent most of his life living in his big brother's shadow ... Comparisons were inevitable. It seemed everyone asked the same questions: Can you skate like the Rocket? Can you score like the Rocket? Can you help the team as much as the Rocket?

Like most younger brothers, the Pocket Rocket resented such comparisons. He was Henri Richard — not Maurice Richard. "What do they expect of me?" he asked. "I am not my brother. He is the greatest hockey player of all time and I don't try to imitate him."

But was there such a big gap between the abilities of the Richard brothers? A press release by NHL statistician Ron Andrews, dated December 2, 1964, poses some interesting comparisons. Issued to announce Henri Richard's 200th career goal on November 28, 1964, this milestone marker came in the 587th game of his career.

Andrews also quoted Maurice, who said, "Henri is a better all-round player than I ever was ... He stickhandles better, controls the puck more, and skates faster. He's better in every way except in goal scoring."

An analysis of the brothers' scoring stats after each had played 587 games sheds some interesting light on Maurice's comments. Although the Rocket had scored 329 goals compared to Henri's 200, the two were almost even in total points accumulated to that point. Maurice had amassed 546 points; Henri had totalled 545 points.

Near the end of his career Henri received the ultimate compliment. After years of playing in the shadow of his older and more famous brother, future Hall of Fame coach Scotty Bowman, then the coach of the Canadiens, in a 1974 article said that Henri "… is a complete hockey player … Maybe a more complete hockey player in some respects than Maurice 'Rocket' Richard …"

And indeed, he did not need to imitate anyone. Henri Richard's career stands as one of the best, on a team that boasts countless superstars throughout its history. Twice he led the NHL in assists. Henri scored over 50 points in 14 different seasons, and he was the ninth player to surpass the 1,000 career-points marker. Richard was recognized as an all-star on four occasions. In 1958 he was named to the First All Star Team. He garnered Second All Star Team status in 1959, 1961, and 1963.

Henri Richard retired at the end of the 1974–1975 season. That same year he was awarded the Bill Masterton Trophy for perseverance, sportsmanship, and dedication to the game of hockey.

Chapter 9
Milt Schmidt: One of the Kitchener Kids

NHL president Clarence Campbell spoke these words in 1951 when he presented Milt Schmidt with the Hart Trophy as the NHL's Most Valuable Player:

"Milt Schmidt typifies everything that a hockey player should be. He has heart, courage, speed, ability and color, and provides inspiration to his team."

Schmidt was recognized as the league's Most Valuable Player after a season of playing with a severely damaged elbow that affected the use of his right arm. During the 1949–1950 season he had suffered an injury to his right elbow. For one reason or another, the arm did not heal properly and he could not lift his right arm above his head. But, with the Bruins in the thick of a battle with the Rangers and the Canadiens for a playoff berth, Schmidt was not about to take any time off. Instead, during the month of January 1951 he fired seven goals in six games to keep Boston in the playoff race. An example of Schmidt's fortitude and ability occurred in mid-January 1951 in a game against the Chicago Blackhawks.

Schmidt had scored early in the game. Chicago came back to tie the score. In the third period the Bruins came out flying, determined to win the game. In the second minute of play, Dumart, Fisher, and Schmidt broke out of their own end. Woody Dumart passed the puck to Dunc Fisher. Just as Schmidt was about to break around defenceman Lee Fogolin, Fisher laid a perfect pass onto his stick. In one motion the big centre jumped past the defenceman, who had been caught flat-footed. Faster than sight, Schmidt tucked the puck into the net behind a startled Harry Lumley. The Blackhawks had been beaten twice by a one-armed man!

Milton Conrad "Milt" Schmidt was born on March 5, 1918, in Kitchener, Ontario. In an interview with Kevin Shea for the *Legends of Hockey* website, Schmidt recalled a child-hood incident. He was spending a lot of time playing street and pond hockey. When he was called into the principal's office he was chastised for not paying enough attention to his school work. When Mr. Bain, the principal, asked, "What is ever going to become of you?" the youngster replied, "I'm going to become a professional hockey player."

Schmidt's journey toward a career in professional hockey began at the age of nine when he joined the King Edward School team. His love of the game led to a job selling peanuts at the Queen Street Auditorium during junior hockey games. Interestingly, one day in the not-too-distant future he would be on the other side of the rink boards.

Schmidt played junior hockey in his home town of Kitchener with the Greenshirts. He was only 14 years old when he first suited up with the local club. Schmidt played on a line with Bobby Bauer and Woodrow "Woody" Dumart. When he was offered a spot on a junior club in Toronto, the Kitchener club offered Schmidt $10 a week and found him a job that paid 42 cents an hour to keep him from leaving the team. Schmidt accepted Kitchener's offer because it would allow him to stay with his family and contribute financial support to his parents.

Schmidt still has strong ties to his home town of Kitchener. He returns frequently and in a 2001 interview with the *Kitchener Record* he said that he always drives by the house on Shanley Street where he grew up.

The Boston Bruins signed Bobby Bauer in 1935 and then inked Woody Dumart to a contact. The two linemates convinced Bruins' coach and general manager Art Ross to invite their centre, Schmidt, to training camp.

Schmidt had originally caught the eye of the Toronto Maple Leafs. But they felt that although he was tall enough, he was too lightweight to withstand the rigors of the National Hockey League. There were also concerns about his fragility,

Milt Schmidt

probably because he had broken his collarbone three times in junior hockey. When Ross sent Schmidt a letter inviting him to training camp, he received a surprising acceptance letter from the youngster. In the letter Schmidt told Ross that he would work hard all summer to earn enough money to pay his way to camp. Ross immediately let the youngster know that the Bruins would pay his way. After training camp ended

Ross gave Schmidt a new pair of skates and told him to go home and concentrate on gaining some weight. Ross wanted the 125-pound "drain pipe thin" Schmidt to be able to endure the pounding that he would take once he made the NHL.

Later in his career Ross probably was proud of his early assessment of Schmidt's abilities. He once stated, "Schmidt was the fastest playmaker of all time. No player ever skated at the tilt the way he did and was still able to make a play." And, Ross continued to say that Schmidt was "one of the best body-checking forwards ever to play in the NHL." Despite his aggressive style he never accumulated more than 57 penalty minutes in a season.

The three friends from the Greenshirts were assigned to Boston's minor league club in Providence at the start of the 1936–1937 season. While they were playing in Providence they were given the moniker the Kraut Line. According to *Legends of Hockey* website, Providence coach Albert Leduc referred to them as "the Krauts" because all three were of German heritage.

Midway through the 1936–1937 season Schmidt was called up to the NHL and his linemates joined him for the last game of the season. In his first full season in the NHL Schmidt earned a salary of $3,500. In this era of million dollar salaries it is hard to imagine that as a Hall of Fame centre Schmidt never earned more than $20,000 in a season!

During the 1938–1939 season Schmidt tallied 15 goals and 17 assists. But in the playoffs he and his linemates really clicked. Schmidt's scoring prowess continued into the next season. In the 1939–1940 season, Schmidt won the Art Ross Trophy for leading the NHL scoring race and his wingers finished second and third in the scoring race. This was the first time in NHL history that a line had finished 1–2–3 in scoring. (A decade later, Detroit's famed Production Line of Ted Lindsay, Sid Abel, and Gordie Howe would duplicate this feat.)

Schmidt was a powerful, hard-hitting centre who never gave up the puck without a fight. Although he was a centre he often used his size to force his way into the opponent's end along boards rather than skating down the centre of the ice. Consequently, he suffered many injuries during the course of his career including a broken jaw, torn rib cartilage, and ligament damage to both knees.

He played with the Bruins until midway through the 1954–1955 campaign when he retired to become the club's coach. Schmidt missed three seasons during World War II. But even though he was enlisted in the RCAF, he still played for the Allen Cup champion, the Ottawa Hurricanes.

Because of the war with Germany, the line's nickname was no longer considered appropriate, and a contest was held in Boston to come up with a new moniker for the trio. The winning entry was the Buddy Line. They were also known for a short time as the Kitchener Kids. But despite these efforts to change their nickname, Schmidt, Dumart, and Bauer were never able to get away from their familiar, original nickname of the Kraut Line.

Schmidt was injury plagued throughout the 1940–1941 regular season, but once the playoffs began he stepped up his performance to high gear. He was the leading scorer, notching five goals and six assists, and leading the Bruins past Toronto and Detroit to capture the Stanley Cup.

In January 1942 all three members of the Kraut Line left the Bruins to join the Royal Canadian Air Force. Schmidt often stated that the biggest night of his hockey career occurred on January 10, 1942. This game against the Montreal Canadiens was the last time the line played together in the National Hockey League before joining the air force. It was an event to remember. Boston defeated Montreal 8–1 and the Kraut Line combined for 8 points. At the end of the game players from both teams hoisted Schmidt, Bauer, and Dumart on their shoulders, carrying them off the ice while the organist played "Auld Lang Sine." As Schmidt later recalled, "A man couldn't ever forget a thing like that."

Although Schmidt's arrival to the NHL had been delayed because he was considered too frail for the league, he amply demonstrated his toughness throughout his career. Perhaps his dedication to the team and willingness to overcome adversity were best illustrated by events in the latter half of the 1950–1951 year. Schmidt had injured his elbow the previous season. In January 1951, when the Bruins were embroiled in the playoff race, Schmidt's elbow was so sore he could not lift his arm above his head. Nevertheless, in the space of six games he scored seven goals, four of which were game winners. The once-frail youngster had developed into one of the toughest centres in the National Hockey League.

Bob Goldham, a rugged defenceman who played against Schmidt and later became a television hockey analyst, had high praise for Schmidt. In an interview he said, "You can have Jean Béliveau and Gretzky and the rest. None of them went all-out like Schmidt. He didn't need a bodyguard; he took care of himself."

Goldham further illustrated Schmidt's toughness and unwillingness to back down from anyone. Jack "Black Jack" Stewart was one of the toughest defencemen in the league in the 1940s and early 1950s. When Stewart was a teammate of Goldham's in Detroit, the big defenceman would tell his Red Wings teammates not to bother about Schmidt. He would announce to the dressing room before the game, "Okay, gentlemen. Don't forget, tonight number 15 [Schmidt] is mine". And, Goldham recalled the same was being said in the Bruins' dressing room. When the game began, it was all-out war between the two, with Stewart doing anything he could to keep Schmidt from scoring and the Boston centre retaliating just as aggressively.

Many years after he retired Schmidt remembered his ongoing feud with Stewart. He recalled how odd it was during the 1948 All Star game to have Black Jack as his teammate. "I remember how strange it felt for me to be dressing in the same room with Jack, shaking hands, and wearing the same colours."

But things returned to normal once the All Star game was over. On November 7th the Red Wings played the Bruins. On his first rush into the Detroit end, Schmidt and Stewart got into a high sticking duel. No penalties were called. Later in the game, Schmidt roared into the Red Wings' end and Stewart came out to meet him. Like a runaway freight train, Schmidt crashed right through the Detroit defenceman. When the play left the Red Wings' zone, Stewart chased after Schmidt and slammed him into the boards. Immediately the Bruin centre came off the boards swinging at his old nemesis. Both were sent off with penalties.

Playing on the All Star Team with rivals did not sit well with the combative Schmidt. Although he appreciated being selected to the All Star Team, and counted each opportunity as a personal career highlight, he commented that once that game was over, his all-star teammates had better keep their heads up, or he would run them over.

Although he didn't mind playing hockey with an edge, Schmidt was always ready to run over an opponent if necessary to get the job down. He also appreciated players who played hard but clean hockey. In a Milt Dunnell column in the *Toronto Star*, Schmidt was reported to have said that he most enjoyed playing against Maple Leafs' star Syl Apps. He said, "When you played against Apps, you knew he was out there to play hockey. That gave *you* a chance to play hockey. You didn't have to spend three-quarters of your time defending yourself."

Howie Meeker recalled in his memoirs, *Golly Gee – It's*

Milt Schmidt: One of the Kitchener Kids

Me!: The Howie Meeker Story, that "you couldn't run Milt; he ran you!" But Meeker said that although Schmidt was tough, he was also a tremendous skater and finesse player. Schmidt used to "wind up in his own end with the puck and, just like Bobby Orr, he'd come out from behind the net on an angle, take two crossover steps into high speed, and would be gone like a jet."

Schmidt won the Hart Trophy as the league's Most Valuable Player in 1951–1952. Three times he was selected to the First All Star Team and once to the Second All Star Team.

Although Bobby Bauer had retired from the National Hockey League in 1947, he returned to Boston for a game on March 18, 1952. That was the night his two friends and former linemates, Schmidt and Dumart, were to be honoured. Before the game the three were presented with gold watches and other gifts. To cap the festivities, early in the game Bauer passed the puck to Dumart at centre ice. Dumart roared in on the Chicago net, firing a hard shot that was blocked. However, the ever-vigilant Schmidt banged in the rebound to score the 200th goal of his NHL career.

During the 1954–1955 season, Schmidt's playing career came to an abrupt end when he retired to become the coach of the Bruins. With the exception of the 1960–1961 season, Schmidt coached Boston until 1966. He also served as the club's general manager, engineering the blockbuster trade that brought Phil Esposito and Ken Hodge to the Bruins. It was during his tenure that Bobby Orr became a Boston Bruin.

In 1961 Milt Schmidt was elected to the Hockey Hall of Fame, and in 1996 he was honoured with the Lester Patrick Award for his efforts to promote the sport of hockey in the United States.

When Boston's general manager Lynn Patrick appointed Schmidt to succeed him as coach of the Bruins, he paid Schmidt a tremendous compliment. He said, "Schmidt will never be as successful as I was as coach [because] he'll never be able to look down the bench when the team's in trouble and holler as I could, 'Milt, get out there!'"

But perhaps a much greater tribute was given to Schmidt by former referee and Hall of Fame member Red Storey. In Dan Diamond's book, *Ultimate Hockey*, Storey named an all-time all-star team as follows: Bill Durnan in goal, King Clancy and Eddie Shore on defence, Howie Morenz at centre, with Gordie Howe and Ted Lindsay on the wings. Then he said, "Now I'll pick you another team that'd knock the socks off that one ... Give me five Milt Schmidts up front and put your grandmother in goal and we'd never lose."

Chapter 10
Ralph Weiland:
A Harvard Man

Hockey was Ralph Weiland's life. Like most youngsters, when he was not on the river or pond playing shinny for hours on end, he was dreaming of playing professional hockey.

Ralph "Cooney" Weiland was born in Egmondville, a small hamlet outside the town of Seaforth in southwestern Ontario, on November 5, 1904. Life was not easy for a youngster growing up in a family of nine children — eight boys and a girl. Weiland's father was a cooper who made and repaired barrels at a local sawmill. Ralph's childhood was spent attending school and playing hockey. But it was not long before hockey dominated his life and he left school to work at the same sawmill as his father. But more importantly, leaving school meant that he had more time to play hockey on the nearby Bayfield River. He was the original "rink rat," but since his rinks were the outdoor rinks provided by nature, his friends called him River Rat.

When he finally left home to pursue his dream, who would have guessed that Weiland would fulfil the dreams of countless young Canadian boys and achieve pinnacles of success that were far beyond the imagination? In a somewhat ironic turn of fate, this Canadian farm boy who, as a youngster, was far more interested in pursuing a career in hockey than furthering his education, ended up making a dramatic impact at one of the most hallowed educational institutions in the world.

Weiland left home to play junior hockey in Owen Sound, Ontario. In 1924, his second year in that Georgian Bay port community, he led the Greys to the Memorial Cup championship. Following his junior career he played minor professional hockey in Minnesota before joining the Boston Bruins. As a Bruin he set league scoring records and led the club to two Stanley Cups. When his playing days ended, Weiland became the coach of the Bruins and led his club to another Stanley Cup. He left the National Hockey League to continue his coaching career with Harvard University. His contributions to American college hockey were recognized when he was awarded the Lester Patrick Award for outstanding contributions to the sport of hockey in the United States.

At first Weiland played for the local team, the Seaforth Highlanders, but his quest for a career in professional hockey meant leaving home to play at a higher level. In 1922, the young Weiland made his way north to Owen Sound on Georgian Bay to tryout for the Owen Sound Greys junior club. This move would prove to be an important turning point for him.

In 1924, Weiland and linemate Melville "Butch" Keeling, who would later star for the New York Rangers, led the Greys to a Memorial Cup championship. It was while he was with the Greys that he first received the adulation of hockey fans. Many men who grew up in Owen Sound at the time remember skating on the harbour ice pretending that they were Ralph Weiland or "Butch" Keeling. In fact, one Owen Sound family named their pet rabbits after Weiland and his teammates!

Weiland's fame in Owen Sound was well earned. He scored 33 goals during the 1923–1924 regular season. But in the playoffs he excelled, notching 37 goals in 15 games to lead the Greys to their first Memorial Cup.

The Memorial Cup championship proved to be his springboard to success. The following season he inked a contract with the Minnesota Rockets of the United States Hockey League. After one season with the Rockets, Weiland signed with the Minneapolis Millers.

In 1928 Weiland's boyhood dream came true when he was signed by the Boston Bruins. He was of small stature, but with two six-foot tall wingers, Dit Clapper and Norman "Dutch" Gainor, the troika was given the moniker the Dynamite Line. And explosive they were!

In the 1928 Stanley Cup final against the New York

Rangers, the rookie shone. In game one of the series he scored two goals, including the game winner, and an assist in Boston's victory. The second game of the three game final series was played in New York and once again "Cooney" shone in a 5–1 victory. He notched four goals, including the game and series winner.

In their second season together, 1929–1930, Clapper netted 41 goals and Weiland set a league scoring record with 43 goals in 44 games. These goals, added to 30 assists, gave him the league scoring title. His 73 points established a new record for the NHL. This was an astounding number when one considers that the previous season high for points had been the 61 amassed by the legendary Howie Morenz.

In 1932, due to differences between himself and Art Ross, coach and general manager of the Boston Bruins, Weiland was traded to Ottawa. He led the Senators in scoring. But, part way through the 1933–1934 season the financially troubled Ottawa team sold him to the Detroit Red Wings, where he formed a fearsome line with Red Wings' stars Larry Aurie and Herbie Lewis. On July 11, 1935, with fences mended in Boston, the Bruins reacquired Weiland. He remained there until he retired in 1939 after winning another Stanley Cup, and took over as Bruins' coach the following season. In 1941, he led the Bruins to another Cup title, becoming the only Bruin in the history of the franchise to win a Stanley Cup as both a player and a coach. Interestingly, one of the young boys who had idolized Cooney when he played for the Owen

Sound Greys, Pat McReavy, was a member of that Stanley Cup winning team in Boston.

After this successful season Weiland left the NHL to become the coach of Hershey in the American Hockey League, a position that he held until 1945. In 1950 he became the head coach of Harvard University's hockey team. Weiland remained in this position for more than two decades until he retired in 1971. During his long tenure behind the Harvard bench he was twice honoured (1954–1955 and 1970–1971) with the Spencer T. Penrose Award as the Coach of the Year in United States College Hockey.

In 1971, Ralph "Cooney" Weiland was inducted into the Hockey Hall of Fame. His already impressive resume included the 1924 Memorial Cup, two Stanley Cups (1928–1929 and 1938–1939) as a player and one Cup as a coach (1940–1941), and a league scoring record. But that was not the end of the accolades. The next year, 1972, he was honoured with the prestigious Lester Patrick Trophy for outstanding contributions to the game of hockey in the United States.

Not a bad career for a Canadian boy who grew up skating on the ponds and rivers in a tiny rural village in southwestern Ontario!

Chapter 11
Fred Taylor:
Cyclone

Although this book is about great centres in the history of professional hockey, it would be remiss to ignore Fred "Cyclone" Taylor, who was one of the greatest hockey players of all time in a position that no longer exists in the sport — rover. The rover was the seventh man on the ice. His responsibilities were similar to those of a centre. In fact, one could argue that the rover was just another centre ice player. His responsibilities ranged across the width and length of the ice surface. Just as the name implies, rovers ranged all over the ice, having both offensive and defensive responsibilities.

Taylor was born in Tara, Ontario, a small farming community about 24 kilometres west of the city of Owen Sound, on June 23, 1884 (some sources list his birth date as June

24, 1884). When Fred was seven years old the Taylor family moved to Listowel, Ontario.

He played most of his minor hockey in Listowel, but it was in Tara that he got his start as a hockey player and, more importantly, as an extremely fast skater.

Petty larceny was involved in his first skating attempts when, at the age of five, he stole his sister's skates and headed to the nearest sheet of ice to try them out. Cyclone later recalled, "I pinched my sister's skates ... I got the dickens for it afterward, but it was worth it."

Once he tried skating he was hooked. The youngster spent all his time skating on the ponds, river, and rinks in Tara. His love of skating and hockey came to the attention of Jack Rigg, a barber in Tara. Rigg was a well-known speed skater and Taylor credited Rigg with teaching him to speed skate.

Taylor's prowess as a hockey player led him to teams and leagues where the other players were much older and much larger than he was. His mother worried about her young son being injured. Because of her concerns, Mrs. Taylor may have been one of the inventors of protective hockey pads. To help her young son avoid injuries, she sewed layers of felt into his long underwear, providing a buffer against stick, puck, and bodycheck injuries. Soon other players were putting such padding into their underwear, too.

Cyclone was involved in a few controversies during his career. One of his earlier exploits occurred in 1903 when he began his junior career in Listowel at the age of 13, playing for the Listowel Mintos. Bill Hewitt, the father of famous sports broadcaster Foster Hewitt, became enamoured of Taylor's talents and approached him about joining his club, the Toronto Marlboros. Taylor refused Hewitt's overtures. This proved not to be a prudent action on the young player's part. Hewitt, who was not used to being turned down, went to the Ontario Hockey Association and successfully had Taylor blacklisted by that organization.

This action did not deter Taylor's hockey aspirations, nor did it lead him to accept Hewitt's offer to play with the Marlboros. Instead, he moved west in 1904 and signed a contract with a team in northern Michigan.

In Houghton-Portage Lakes, Taylor was far from the jurisdiction of the amateur Ontario Hockey Association, since the International Professional Hockey League that he was now skating in was professional. In fact, it was the first and only professional hockey league in existence at the time. His first professional contract called for a monthly salary of $25 and free room and board.

In 1907, the International Hockey League ceased to operate and Taylor found himself without a team for the 1907–1908 season. But his hockey unemployment did not last long. He signed a contract to play for the Ottawa Senators.

It was while he was playing in the nation's capital that he acquired the moniker Cyclone. There are many stories about how the nickname came about. Certainly, one of the most intriguing involves the governor general of Canada.

Fred Taylor: Cyclone

The legend goes that Earl Grey, who was a huge sports fan, happened to be at the first game Taylor played for the Ottawa Senators. His blazing speed dazzled both players and fans alike, and when he used it to dominate the game, scoring five goals in his very first game in the league, it was reported that the governor general turned to his aide and commented, "They should call that man the Cyclone — his speed blew the other team out of the rink." From that point forth, the story goes, he was called Cyclone Taylor. (Oddly enough, in Michigan he'd been known as a whirlwind.)

After a couple of seasons with Ottawa, Taylor made a move that once again would embroil him in controversy. He left the Senators to play for their arch rivals, the Renfrew Millionaires. Because of the close geographical proximity between Ottawa and Renfrew, Cyclone's defection made the Senators' fans irate and gave the Ottawa media plenty of fodder for the sports columns.

The date, February 12, 1910, was etched in the minds of the entire Ottawa sports community. Cyclone Taylor and his Renfrew Millionaires would be in town to play the Senators. Before the game Taylor responded to his vilification in the media and by the Ottawa fans by pronouncing that he would skate backwards through the entire Ottawa team and score a goal!

He did just that! Or did he? Taylor did score a goal on a backhanded shot. But did he skate through the entire Senators team backwards? Ottawa fans said that he failed to keep his boast. Others at the game claimed that he did perform such a feat. One of the eyewitnesses who claimed to have seen the event said she was sure that Cyclone had skated through the entire team backwards and scored the goal. This was none other than Charlotte Whitten, who later in life became the flamboyant mayor of Ottawa (one of the first women in Canada to hold such a high elected public position).

But what about Cyclone? What did he claim after the event? To his dying day, Cyclone responded to the question with answers so ambiguous that any politician would have envied his ability to skate around an issue without giving an definitive answer. One fact, however, *was* certain. While Cyclone Taylor played for the Ottawa Senators his salary was second to none when compared with major athletes in all sports of that era. At $5,250 for 12 games, he earned more than the Detroit Tigers paid the greatest baseball player of the time, Ty Cobb. Taylor is considered by many to be hockey's first superstar.

In 1912 Taylor left Renfrew to join the Vancouver Millionaires of the Pacific Coast Hockey League. But he continued to rub salt into an old wound when, in 1915, he led his team to the Stanley Cup championship by defeating his former club, the Ottawa Senators. In the three game final, Cyclone notched six goals against his old team.

During this early era of hockey a great goal scorer might notch 20 goals in a season. Taylor's scoring totals were truly amazing for his time. In nine seasons playing in the Pacific

Fred Taylor: Cyclone

Coast Hockey League he notched 213 goals and was credited with 118 assists. To make these numbers even more remarkable, he played a mere 169 games during the nine seasons of his west coast career. Cyclone played only a few games more, in his entire career, than a modern-day player will play in two seasons! On average, Taylor scored 1.26 goals per game, for his entire career.

He scored more than 500 points playing for Ottawa, Renfrew, and Vancouver. This is a remarkable total during a time in which era assists were often not recorded. One can only imagine what his point totals might be in comparison to Wayne Gretzky, Gordie Howe, and the other great scorers of the modern era if more attention had been paid to assist totals and more accurate records had been maintained.

Frank Patrick, a hockey legend in his own right, called Cyclone Taylor, "the greatest player I ever saw." This is a strong endorsement when one considers that Patrick ran his own league, instituted 22 rules that are a part of the National Hockey League rule book, built Canada's first artificial ice rink, and was a player as well.

In 1947 the world of hockey paid Cyclone the ultimate hockey player's honour when he was elected as an honoured member of the Hockey Hall of Fame.

Cyclone Taylor is truly an all-star of all time in the world of hockey. From 1900 to 1918, he was named to the First All Star Team in every league in which he played. This is a remarkable feat, indeed!

Acknowledgments

This book could not have been written without the efforts and support of many people. Craig Campbell and his staff at the Hockey Hall of Fame were, as always, most supportive in finding information and photos for the book. Kevin Shea's "One on One" interviews, found on the Hockey Hall of Fame's website, were also of great assistance.

Staff members in the reference department at the main branch of the Kitchener Public Library were extremely helpful in finding information about their native son, Milt Schmidt. The Society for International Hockey Research website database provided a wealth of information that helped in the verification of information gathered elsewhere.

My editor, Deborah Lawson, and the editorial staff at Altitude Publishing, were always available to answer my questions and provide necessary editorial input.

My brother, David, made available his vast collection of hockey periodicals for my research needs. My nephew, Sean Illman White, was always a wealth of ideas and inspiration during the writing of this book. My father, who has been an ardent hockey fan for most of his 80 years, provided me with his personal insights on the players featured in this book. In fact, both of my parents are a constant source of encouragement and I appreciate them very much.

Finally, I would like to thank my wife, Judy, for her encouragement and support, which included reading and commenting on several versions of the draft.

Photo Credits

Cover: Bruce Bennet Studios/Getty Images. Imperial Oil-Turofsky/Hockey Hall of Fame: pages 20, 65, 87, 99, 119. Frank Prazak/Hockey Hall of Fame: page 43.

Bibliography

Batten, Jack. *The Leafs*. Toronto: Key Porter Books, 1994.

Béliveau, Jean, with Chrys Goyens and Allan Turowetz. *Jean Béliveau: My Life in Hockey*. Toronto: McClelland & Stewart Inc., 1994.

Diamond, Dan, and Associates. *Ultimate Hockey*. New York: Total Sports, 1998.

Geoffrion, Bernard and Stan Fischler. *Boom Boom: The Life and Times of Bernard Geoffrion*. Toronto: McGraw-Hill Ryerson, 1997.

Goyens, Chrys and Allan Turowetz. *Lions in Winter*. Scarborough, Ontario: Prentice Hall Canada Inc., 1986.

Hockey Hall of Fame Internet website
http://www.hhof.com/index.htm

Hornby, Lance. *Hockey's Greatest Moments: Celebrating the Best In Hockey*. Toronto: Key Porter Books, 2004.

Bibliography

Leonetti, Mike. *The Game We Knew: Hockey in the Fifties.* Vancouver: Raincoast Books, 1997.

Meeker, Howie. *Golly Gee – It's Me!: The Howie Meeker Story* Toronto: Stoddart Publishing Company Ltd., 1996.

Mouton, Claude. *The Montreal Canadiens.* Toronto: Van Nostrand Reinhold Ltd., 1980.

Podnieks, Andrew. *Players: The Ultimate A-Z Guide of Everyone Who Has Ever Played in the NHL.* Toronto: Doubleday Canada, 2003.

Shea, Kevin. *Barilko: Without a Trace.* Bolton: Fenn Publishing Company Ltd., 2004.

Weir, Glen, Jeff Chapman, and Travis Weir. *Ultimate Hockey.* Toronto: Stoddart Publishing Company, 1999.

Young, Scott. *Conn Smythe: If You Can't Beat 'Em in the Alley.* Toronto: McClelland and Stewart, 1981.

Articles

Claassen, Harold. "The Kraut Line." *Inside Hockey*, Winter 1967–1968.

Cuomo, Pete. "The Subtle Greatness that is Alex Delvecchio." *Hockey Illustrated*, March 1970.

Foss, Steve. "Henri Richard — Misunderstood Canadien Hero." *Hockey*, January 1974.

MacLean, Norman. "Henri Richard At the Crossroads." *Hockey Illustrated*, December 1967.

Rimstead, Paul. "The Best That Ever Came Down the Pike." *Star Weekly: The Canadian Magazine*, April 6-20, 1968.

Sisti, Tony. "Saga of the Richards." *Inside Hockey*, Winter 1967–1968.

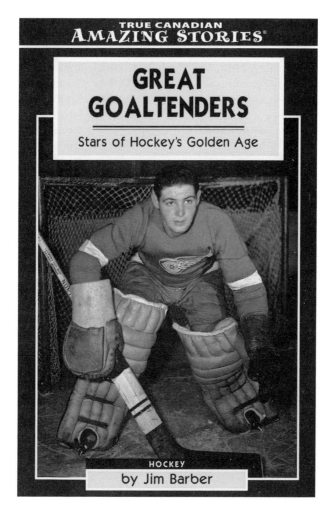

OTHER AMAZING STORIES

These titles are available wherever you buy books. If you have trouble finding the book you want, call the Altitude order desk at **1-800-957-6888**, e-mail your request to: **orderdesk@altitudepublishing.com** or visit our Web site **at www.amazingstories.ca**

New **AMAZING STORIES** titles are published every month.